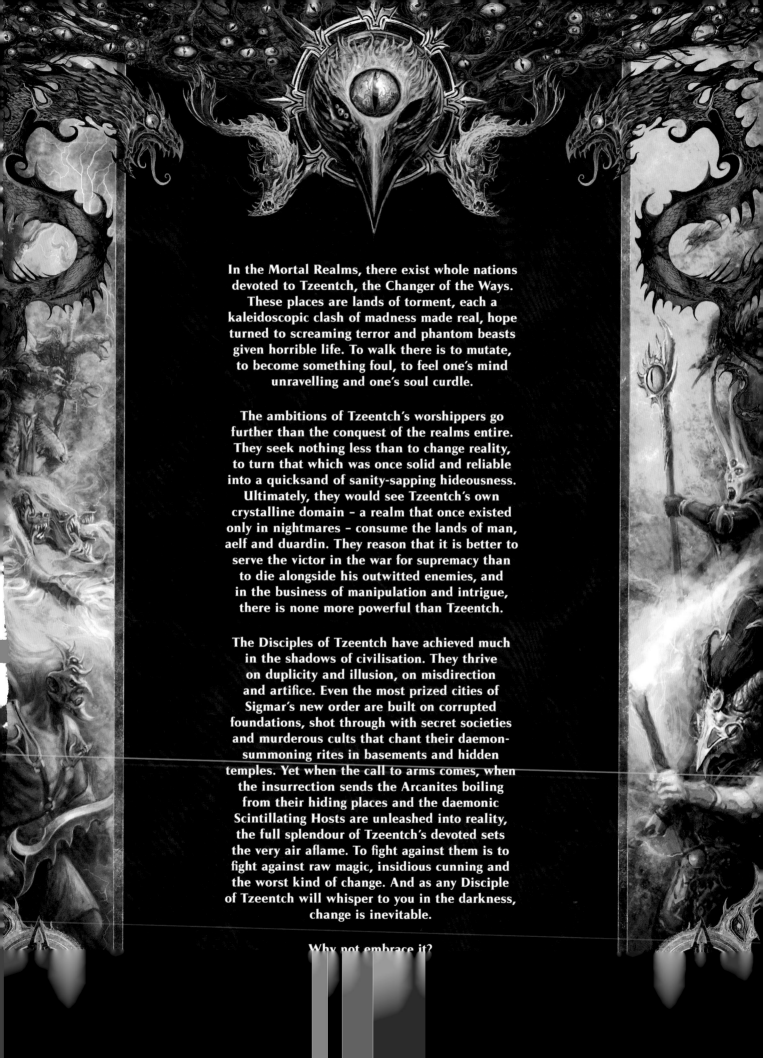

In the Mortal Realms, there exist whole nations
devoted to Tzeentch, the Changer of the Ways.
These places are lands of torment, each a
kaleidoscopic clash of madness made real, hope
turned to screaming terror and phantom beasts
given horrible life. To walk there is to mutate,
to become something foul, to feel one's mind
unravelling and one's soul curdle.

The ambitions of Tzeentch's worshippers go
further than the conquest of the realms entire.
They seek nothing less than to change reality,
to turn that which was once solid and reliable
into a quicksand of sanity-sapping hideousness.
Ultimately, they would see Tzeentch's own
crystalline domain – a realm that once existed
only in nightmares – consume the lands of man,
aelf and duardin. They reason that it is better to
serve the victor in the war for supremacy than
to die alongside his outwitted enemies, and
in the business of manipulation and intrigue,
there is none more powerful than Tzeentch.

The Disciples of Tzeentch have achieved much
in the shadows of civilisation. They thrive
on duplicity and illusion, on misdirection
and artifice. Even the most prized cities of
Sigmar's new order are built on corrupted
foundations, shot through with secret societies
and murderous cults that chant their daemon-
summoning rites in basements and hidden
temples. Yet when the call to arms comes, when
the insurrection sends the Arcanites boiling
from their hiding places and the daemonic
Scintillating Hosts are unleashed into reality,
the full splendour of Tzeentch's devoted sets
the very air aflame. To fight against them is to
fight against raw magic, insidious cunning and
the worst kind of change. And as any Disciple
of Tzeentch will whisper to you in the darkness,
change is inevitable.

Why not embrace it?

CONTENTS

THE ELDRITCH THREAT. . 4

TZEENTCH ALMIGHTY. 8

THE CRYSTAL LABYRINTH . .10

DOMAINS OF THE CULTS. . . .12

THE CHILDREN
OF CHANGE. 14

THE SCINTILLATING
HOSTS 16
The Flesh Ascended 17
Nine Shall Be Their Number. . . . 18

TZEENTCH ARCANITES 20
The Arch Conspirators. 22
Secrets of the Cults. 24
The Marks of Change. 26

SKEINS OF FATE AFLAME . . .28
Lords of Change 30
Heralds of Tzeentch 32
Favoured Scions of Tzeentch . . . 34
Bestial Agents of Change. 35
Horrors of Tzeentch 36
Mortal Masters of the Arcane. . . 38
Lords of the Silver Towers 40
Tzaangors. 42

THE ELDRITCH HOST. . . 46

MAGIC AND MUTATION 58

PAINTING YOUR
DISCIPLES OF TZEENTCH . . .60

DISCIPLES OF
TZEENTCH 68

ALLEGIANCE ABILITIES. 69
Battle Traits 69
Command Traits. 72
Artefacts of Power 74
Spell Lores 76
The Eternal Conflagration. 78
The Hosts Duplicitous 79
The Hosts Arcanum 80
The Cult of the
Transient Form 81
The Pyrofane Cult. 82
The Guild of Summoners 83
Battleplan:
The Concealed Cultist 84

PATH TO GLORY 86
Tzeentch Warband Tables. 88

WARSCROLLS 90
Fate Legion. 90
Warpflame Host 92
Multitudinous Host 92
Aether-eater Host 92
Change Host 93
Overseer's Fate-twisters. 93
Omniscient Oracles 93
Arcanite Cult. 94
Arcanite Cabal 96
Alter-kin Coven 96
Witchfyre Coven. 96
Skyshoal Coven 97
Tzaangor Coven 97
Lord of Change 98
Kairos Fateweaver. 99

Gaunt Summoner
of Tzeentch. 100
Fateskimmer, Herald of
Tzeentch on Burning Chariot. . 101
Fluxmaster, Herald of
Tzeentch on Disc. 102
The Changeling. 103
Changecaster,
Herald of Tzeentch 103
The Blue Scribes 104
Screamers of Tzeentch 104
Burning Chariots
of Tzeentch. 105
Exalted Flamers of Tzeentch. . . 106
Flamers of Tzeentch 106
Horrors of Tzeentch 107
Magister on Disc of Tzeentch . . 108
Magister 109
Curseling, Eye of Tzeentch 109
The Eyes of the Nine. 110
Vortemis the All-Seeing 110
Fatemaster 111
Ogroid Thaumaturge 111
Kairic Acolytes 112
Tzaangor Skyfires 113
Tzeentch Chaos Spawn 113
Tzaangor Shaman. 114
Tzaangor Enlightened 115
Tzaangor Enlightened
on Discs of Tzeentch 115
Tzaangors. 116
Burning Sigil of Tzeentch 117
Tome of Eyes 117
Daemonic Simulacrum 118

PITCHED BATTLE
PROFILES 119

PRODUCED BY THE WARHAMMER STUDIO
With thanks to The Faithful for their additional playtesting services.

Games Workshop Ltd., Willow Road, Lenton, Nottingham, NG7 2WS, United Kingdom
games-workshop.com

The cold, shadowy landscape of Ulgu suddenly explodes into a riot of colour as a Tzaangor tribe summons a host of Tzeentchian daemons, their mutagenic energy ravaging the land itself.

THE ELDRITCH THREAT

While the crude warlords of the mortal races measure their success by territory conquered, the Disciples of Tzeentch seek nothing less than to capsize reality itself. They are masters of the sorcerous rite and the devious plot. When at war, a barrage of magic reveals the awful truth – that their enemies were doomed before the first shot was fired.

The skies burn livid pink and cerulean blue. Trees writhe and become tentacled horrors. The land cracks to form needle-fanged mouths that scream in protest, for such intense concentrations of magic are unnatural even in the enchanted reaches of the Mortal Realms. The Disciples of Tzeentch have shucked off their illusions and gone to war en masse, and with them comes the terrible truth: the realms belong more to the scions of the Chaos Gods than they do to those races that defy them.

The Disciples of Tzeentch are neither simple warriors nor brawlers, nor are they mercenaries or soldiers of fortune; they train but rarely with the sword and the bow, and they spurn the cannon and the gun. Nor do they study the treatises of warmasters and conquerors from ages past. To them, such conventional conceits, such everyday tools of battle, are as crass and simplistic as the daubings of a child upon a father's masterpiece. To these devotees of change, the notion of war is mutable in the extreme, as is the flesh and mindscape of the foe. They fight their battles on several planes at once – the mental, the spiritual and the physical all mingling together into one mind-boggling and spectacular whole.

Tzeentch's devoted are steeped in matters arcane. Through long study and diabolical pact, their understanding of the nature of things is so advanced that they can shape reality. With an arrhythmical chant or a carefully inscribed phrase given voice, they conjure bolts of wyrdfire that can strip a man's flesh from his bones or melt stone to the consistency of butter. Some can peer into the future or squint into the murky mists of the past, plucking secrets from the pliant branches of fate that they have bent to their will. To fight them is maddening, for to land a solid strike against such an enemy is nigh impossible.

THE MANY FATES OF TZEENTCH

The Mortal Realms were once beyond the reach of the daemons of the Dark Gods. The natural barriers between the worlds of men and the Realm of Chaos held them at bay, just as a mile-thick glacier of hard ice keeps a prospector from the mineral wealth of the mountain beyond. The far-seeing daemons of Tzeentch could only look on in avaricious frustration as they peered at the Mortal Realms through the fractal reflections of the Crystal Labyrinth. Here were eight complex new realities for them to uncover, corrupt and twist into unrecognisable shapes before claiming them in the name of the Changer of the Ways.

But the Mortal Realms were denied to them by the unyielding lord Sigmar, and they could no more claim them than a swarm of insects could claim the deeps of the sea. Instead, for long ages, they fought their battles in the Realm of Chaos, the Dark Gods matching their might against one another as they worked secret schemes in the background that might one day see their influence expand into pastures new.

However, the daemons of Tzeentch were resourceful in their cunning, and they never truly gave up on their quest to bend new realities to their master's whims. Whenever a mortal mind reached out across the veils of reality through sorcery or shamanistic rite, they would cluster around, eyes wide with glee, and whisper their corrupting truths. Whenever a convoluted ploy saw a schemer lay a rival low, they would gather in the shadows, murmuring of rewards untold should the victor follow the darkness in their soul to its logical conclusion.

It began as a hushed prayer here, an arcane diagram there, but soon – and with gathering speed – the imprecations for Tzeentch's favour became more and more common. The Hanging Valleys saw Anvrok's foremost meteoromancers, who formerly prayed for the gift of fresh water from the skies, make sacrifices to the entity they knew as the God Mercurial – and, in doing so, unwittingly give tribute to Tzeentch. In the courts of Prosperis, those who were bored with their wealthy and privileged lives took up the dark arts in the hope of finding new areas of reality to conquer, for proving their supremacy had become a way of life. They too were rewarded, but they found far more than they bargained for and fell to madness. In Hysh's most remote regions, the scholars that had dared venture into Haixiah begged the skies for the intellect and mental strength necessary to profit from the myriad complex truths that were pouring into their minds. Tzeentch was only too happy to oblige – for a cost, of course – as along with that influx of raw information came a nagging desire to learn the darkest secrets of all.

A whisper, a staring eye, a claw scraping at the mind. Many were the ways that Tzeentch worked at the cracks in reality left by the greed and ambition of mortal men – or, in some places, by the honest need for a simple change of fortune. For the realms are cruel, and there are always those who would seek a better life. On such dreams are the acts of Tzeentch founded.

The daemon hosts first entered the lands of mortals through sites of summonation, having been called from beyond by those who would bind them. Such hermetic conjurations carry a huge degree of risk, however. The daemons of Tzeentch are experts in the arcane arts; magic runs in their blood – or, rather, forms their very substance. They will spot a minute imperfection in a spell or a mangled syllable in the Dark Tongue of a Chaos ritual as eagerly as a miser spots a gold coin in a shallow puddle. Should a would-be daemonologist make such a critical error in his summonations, he may soon find the creature he sought to bind emerging from its ritual circle with a leer of dark glee. The lucky ones are slain soon afterwards, burned to death by warpfire or ripped to pieces by sharp claws. Those less fortunate find themselves the servants rather than the masters, their souls bound forever to the whims of the same arcane forces they hoped to use to their own advantage.

Some of those who sought glory and power from the Architect of Fate are irrevocably changed, bearing iridescent scales, feathered crests or clawed appendages in place of limbs. For the most part, those souls that Tzeentch has claimed for his own bear no mark at all, or else they use glamours and spells to keep the vile aberrations of their form hidden from all save their fellow spellcasters. They labour in secret within the scriptor-houses, colleges and tutelage centres of the free cities, making the most of their daemonic patronage to ascend through society. They then teach new generations the arts of magic as if there were nothing untoward about their pre-eminence – but with ever darker inflections laced through every spell and secret they impart.

Though Tzeentch's claws sunk deep indeed during the Age of Chaos, especially in the ever-shifting Realm of Metal, his ultimate triumph over Chamon has been denied to him by the coming of Sigmar's Tempest. Already, however, the scions of the Changer of the Ways are on the rise once more. The reshaping of the Realm of Death at Nagash's hand has caused the entirety of Shyish to magically invert – a phenomenon that pleases Tzeentch mightily – but more than that, it has spurred a backlash of wild magical energy to roil across the cosmos. To say that the Changer of the Ways had a hand in the coming of the Arcanum Optimar would be an understatement, and he has profited greatly from the intensification of magic that has been unleashed across the lands, seas and skies of the Eight Realms.

Never before have the Disciples of Tzeentch been so well poised for success, as even in his victories, Sigmar has played into his enemy's hands. The spires of progress and civilisation cast long shadows of their own, and in those shadows, anarchy and misrule will thrive…

'*That's them alright,*' *said the Vindicarum Outrider, waving his pistol at the column of tattered refugees in the valley. 'Cultists. Came straight to you, sir, when we found out about 'em.'*
Lord-Castellant Brontos Steelbreaker squinted through the twilight at the traipsing figures. 'Are you sure? They don't look much more than beggars.'
'Tendren and I watched them leave, sir. Saw the tattoos on their ankles. The fish and the serpent entwined, sir, and a nasty glow in the eye.'
Brontos turned to his Judicator-Prime. 'Well?'
Velleros nodded by way of confirmation, unslinging his skybolt bow and nocking a crackling arrow. 'He's right, Brontos. Daemon-touched, one and all.'
'Then we engage, and the reinforcements from Anvilgard can mop up whatever's left,' said the Lord-Castellant, unsheathing his greatblade. 'Hear me? Celestial Vindicators, engage! Charge these traitors!'
Brontos' entire brotherhood of Stormcast Eternals surged forward, voices raised in the song of war as they pounded down the hill towards the refugees below. Bolts of lightning hurtled out from the Judicators on the shoulders of the slopes, only to dissipate metres before impact. The tatterdemalion refugees gave a great shout, shimmering before Brontos' eyes to become tall, athletically built paragons of humanity with grotesque golden masks. Those at the fore sent volleys of strange fire, pink and blue, streaking back towards the Celestial Vindicators. Where they struck, armour ran as molten as quicksilver; some Stormcasts discorporated in blurs

of energy as they returned to the heavens.
At the far side of the column, tangle-horned beastmen made a series of arcane gestures, drawing strange burning runes in the air – and from nothing at all came a spilling, fizzing tide of daemons. Brontos growled, redoubling his pace as fire flew from the creatures' fingers. The first few ranks of Brontos' Liberator phalanxes were consumed by the multicoloured flame, emerging not as burning men but clouds of scintillating crystal butterflies. Then their comrades crashed in, twinned swords hacking, and the true slaughter began.
Though the Stormcasts' sigmarite armour was proof against the blades of the cultists and Tzaangor beastmen, the Vindicarum Freeguilders did not fare so well. Even as Brontos whipped his glaive right and left, letting the righteous wrath consume him, he saw that the Chaos worshippers were concentrating their attacks on his mortal allies rather than the Stormcasts.
Then, all at once, the host of cultists lay hacked apart at his feet. They shimmered as if underwater and became defenceless refugees once more. Brontos looked about himself in confusion, only to see the Anvilgard reinforcements cresting the valley. The newcomers looked upon the carnage, aghast. Many cried out.
With a cold shiver, Brontos stumbled back from the ankle-deep gore around him, realising what the Anvilgard reinforcements must have concluded. They had won a battle this day, but they had lost the wider war.
The sound of daemonic laughter drifted on the wind, but only Brontos, in his wretchedness, could hear it.

The daemonic hosts of Tzeentch burst from arcane portals, ripping their way into reality to assail the Maggotkin of Silker's Ridge. A thousand Arcanite voices are raised in fierce joy as their patrons manifest at the height of their powers, years of careful planning made real – and another swathe of Aqshy claimed for the Great Conspirator.

TZEENTCH ALMIGHTY

The Chaos God Tzeentch is known by many titles, including the Changer of the Ways, the Great Conspirator and the Architect of Fate. Tzeentch's domains are magic, manipulation and guile. He is the god of sorcery as well as deceit – elaborate schemes are his delight, whether they come to fruition or not.

Tzeentch is one of the greater Chaos powers, a brother god to Khorne, Nurgle and Slaanesh, and often a secret ally to the pantheon's newcomer, the Great Horned Rat. Even amongst gods, Tzeentch is the undisputed master of the arcane arts, for magic is the most potent of all agents of change. This does not mean Tzeentch is above sullying his hands with war, rather that he prefers to win battles through guile and sorcery over brute force. The Changer of the Ways favours the cunning over the strong, the manipulative over the violent. A rune-etched stiletto to the heart, perhaps delivered during a sacrificial ritual or by a pseudopod hidden under priestly robes, pleases him far more than the gory battlefield decapitations so beloved of Khorne. Ultimately, though, the act of change is the key element in all that Tzeentch values, and the change between life and death is the most profound of all. The esoteric kill gives him power, an aspect of reality that most of his followers do not fully realise but propagate nonetheless.

In his true shape, Tzeentch is the most outlandish of the Dark Gods. His skin crawls with constantly changing faces that leer and mock any who dare to gaze upon him. As Tzeentch speaks, these faces appear and disappear, some repeating his words with subtle differences or providing mocking commentary to cast doubt upon the original remark. Ever shifting, nothing of Tzeentch feels definitive – even his purpose is

unimaginably complex, his schemes beyond the ken of mortals. He was instrumental in the toppling of the world-that-was into utter destruction and has doomed hundreds of worlds besides, even collapsing realities altogether in those dimensions that once danced to his tune. Now he focuses his myriad eyes on the Mortal Realms, eight more realities for him to toy with. Already one is in his grip.

Tzeentch's growing ascendancy following Sigmar's return to the Mortal Realms and the battles of the Realmgate Wars hints at plans long nursed to fruition. Embedded deep within Sigmar's grand cities, mortal cultists work in secret to advance his unknowable goals, while Tzaangor tribes raid the ancient places of the realms in search of lost treasures and abstruse knowledge. Should the need arise, Tzeentch sends his daemonic hosts forth in all their scintillating glory to sear the land with the coruscating flames of change.

AN ETERNAL RIVALRY

Far beyond the light of sun or star, removed from all reason and reality, lies the Realm of Chaos. There, the Chaos Gods strive against one another in a never-ending power struggle. As one god grows in strength, so do the others conspire against him. Common cause will unite the disparate powers, but even then each god angles to ensure that they emerge from the alliance in a better position than the others. In this endless scheming, none of the gods fare so well as Tzeentch, and he delights in manipulating them all – tormenting ever-raging Khorne or endlessly baiting proud, melodramatic Slaanesh.

However, every Chaos God has his opposite, another whose nature is the antithesis of his own. For Tzeentch, that special foe is Nurgle. The Lord of Decay provides Tzeentch with his fiercest rivalry. Nurgle counters Tzeentch's hope and ambition, his demand for change, with opposing ideologies: a resigned despair that accepts how things are, a willingness not just to be content with the base or mundane but to actually wallow in it. In their unending battles, Tzeentch pits his ceaseless evolution against the stagnant loop of Nurgle's closed cycle of life and death. Tzeentch, who delights in his carefully laid plans, is appalled to watch Nurgle's slovenly and indiscriminate destruction, his jovial attitude to sowing seeds of destruction and letting them grow where they may. The two powers never miss an opportunity to match forces against one another, be it battles over boundaries in the Realm of Chaos, expansionist wars in the Mortal Realms or even scholastic rivalries and cultish intrigues amongst the Cities of Sigmar.

Of late, Tzeentch has gained the upper hand. In Ghyran, where once Nurgle reigned nearly unchallenged, the decaying Kingdom of Bul'ghoh was toppled as a result of the machinations of Kairos Fateweaver. In Chamon's Spiral Crux, Tzeentch has all but eradicated the stain of Nurgle's infections, using a sustained crusade of metallic transmutation that sterilised everything the Grandfather of Plagues had corrupted by disease.

The victories of Tzeentch over Nurgle are by no means confined to the Mortal Realms. In the power struggles fought in the Realm of Chaos, his daemonic minions are usually key to his victories over his brother gods – few mortal agents could stand the sheer inimical otherness of that sinister dimension for long. From beside Nurgle's Great Cauldron itself, the Changeling aided the Blue Scribes in stealing a seven-volume set of tomes listing cures for the Plague God's most potent diseases, and on the borders of Nurgle's Garden, the Swamp of Ages was crystallised during the War of Slime and Fire. Yet just as moons wax and wane, so too does the power balance between the rival gods of Chaos. It does not all go Tzeentch's way – his minions dare not mention the disaster at Lom'nagini or the Night of Cataracted Eyes, during which so many of his daemons were rendered blind by a supernatural plague that for a time Tzeentch himself contracted the same disease.

THE GREAT GAME

The never-ending struggle of each of the Chaos Gods to gain dominion over the others is known as the Great Game, and Tzeentch loves it more dearly than any other pastime. To this most masterful of schemers, this game offers not just endless amusement but also boundless opportunity. Not only does Tzeentch constantly seek to further his own ambitions, he expends just as much of his focus on his desire to manipulate or counteract the best-laid plans of his rivals. Through convoluted stratagems, Tzeentch has subverted his brother gods time and again.

The Realm of Chaos is Tzeentch's playground for the Great Game. There, he instigates infighting, a pursuit of which the god never tires. One of his most infamous deeds in the Great Game was to beguile Khorne's greatest Bloodthirster, Skarbrand, into attacking his patron. It was Tzeentch's magic that finally burned away Nurgle's Ineffable Malady and, although few know the full tale, it was Tzeentch's plotting that led to Slaanesh's capture by the aelven gods and the twist of fate that turned the Dark Prince's ultimate victory into a strange form of defeat. The battles for control of the Mortal Realms have only added new challenges to the Great Game.

Tzeentch's plots may be manifold, but none are simple. Revelling in complexity, Tzeentch's plans can appear contradictory to those few observers able to detect his influence, for he is patient and willing to wait long centuries for his obtuse intrigues to bear fruit. And the Changer of the Ways is fickle, prone to adding elaborate intricacies to his own plots or even introducing obstacles to impede them. Indeed, the Architect of Fate rejoices in the construction of each plan as much as he revels in watching them unravel. Such counter-intuitive twists baffle those who try to understand him, lending an edge of unpredictability to his plots that constantly confounds the foes attempting to pre-empt them.

Across the realms, the Lord of Sorcery spins his impossibly complex webs of secrecy, and servants long embedded in the foundations of Sigmar's realm sow the seeds of madness and fear. Where Khorne and Nurgle seek to destroy and despoil the cities of the God-King, Tzeentch plays a far longer game. In civilisation, there is subtlety, complexity, mechanism and machination. Through cunning and manipulation, the Chaos God's power has blossomed in this age of reason and intrigue. As Sigmar's followers returned to the Mortal Realms, their ranks were infiltrated by daemons and Arcanites using doppelgänger magic, eager to sabotage many of the new cities. Tzeentch's scions, foremost amongst them the Changeling and his fellow trickster-daemons, have led countless of the God-King's faithful astray. Like a spark that ignites an inferno, these daemons have fostered a hundred new cults dedicated to magic, change, knowledge and, ultimately, Tzeentch. By their hand, entire cities have already risen up in rebellion, casting their rulers into the flames of change. Others remain outwardly loyal while heresy and sedition flow through their veins like a cancer, simply waiting for the right moment to strike. Now the time of change draws nearer, and the twisted plans of such entities lead to a confluence of Tzeentch's triumphs.

THE CRYSTAL LABYRINTH

There is nothing that Tzeentch sets his iridescent eyes upon that he does not wish to seize for his own, to control and to manipulate, to change at his whim. So does the Architect of Fate sit at the centre of the Crystal Labyrinth, like a spider on a web, forever hatching plots and sending them forth.

Rivalling Khorne's vast domain in size, the Crystal Labyrinth's shimmering brilliance is a stark contrast to the Blood God's ruddy wastelands. Countless glittering pathways spring from the sprawling maze. Everywhere Horrors scuttle about, using their magics to grow further crystal corridors. Fractal filaments inveigle their way into the dominions of the other gods and, in doing so, bind them all together in a web of causality.

It is a place of mind-bending, sanity-shattering contradictions – even to use the term 'labyrinth' to describe it is to compare the roots of a simple seed to the tangled canopy of an ancient, endless forest caught in the grip of a permanent wildfire. Its corridors and bridges criss-cross through space, time and even thought, alight with magical potential and the energies of raw madness. Only those with the strongest will can negotiate its endless reaches, for the labyrinth's walls reflect hopes, dreams, madness and terror. Those trammelled within come to no physical harm, yet not even those favoured disciples who walk the lands can escape with their minds intact. Impulses of pure change cascade through every league and locale, reordering its dimensions in an endlessly shifting tangle of forms. It is a place that is made of the same impossible substance as its master, and any who attempt to define it find their sanity unravelling fast.

THE IMPOSSIBLE FORTRESS
At the heart of the Labyrinth stands the Impossible Fortress. This is the principal stronghold of Tzeentch himself, and within its contradictory folds and infernal gateways, the Changer of the Ways peers from his myriad eyes into those realities he seeks to bend to his whim. From this nexus of power, he sends impulses, whispers and dreams into the minds of his disciples, guiding them,

goading them and luring them ever further along the paths that lead to either immortal glory or – far likelier – a horrible end.

The exact appearance of the Impossible Fortress changes according to the beholder's aspirations. Some perceive it to be fashioned of the same crystal as the labyrinth that sprawls out around it, whilst others see walls of blue flame, flowing quicksilver or gnarled azure stone. No matter the material, it is always in constant flux. Spires and towers writhe and burst from within its heart, only to collapse and be reabsorbed once more. Gateways, windows and Realmgate portals yawn open like mouths, screaming with cosmic dissonance before closing once more to vanish without trace.

The fortress's innards are no less confounding. Different passages and rooms obey different physical laws or else exist in separate dimensions. What conventional thought deems 'up' in one chamber might be 'down' in another, or even an alternative state of being entirely, such as 'sorrow' or 'the past'. Those trapped inside are soon driven out of their wits, and once they succumb entirely, they collapse into an implosion of thought and form. Such victims are often reborn as familiars, given as both blessing and curse to the champions of Tzeentch in the Eight Realms. There are rumours of one mortal finding a path through the maze and escaping back into the real world – a young girl accompanied by a small dog – though Tzeentch has obfuscated this legend so thoroughly that none can be sure if it is true or if the Changer of the Ways has put the story about in order to lure hopeful travellers to his domain.

Even daemons cannot easily endure the twisted horror of the Impossible Fortress; only the Lords of Change can hope to navigate its corridors

with any degree of success. As a result, no matter how distracted Tzeentch may be by the Great Game, he is never assailed in his stronghold. The other gods have lost too many minions in this way to waste their power again, and hence he is left undisturbed in his maniacal schemes to succeed, fail and confound himself a billion times over and all at the same time.

Scattered across the tangled outer regions of Tzeentch's domain in the Realm of Chaos are nine strongholds arranged in an ever-changing hierarchy – the Fractal Fortresses. Each of these kaleidoscopic spires is home to one of the nine legions, known as the Scintillating Hosts, that Tzeentch favours at any given time, and each is ruled by its most powerful daemon. There, the titular Overseer receives commands from Tzeentch himself and, in turn, relays their own version of those orders outwards to the subordinate convocations, who compete to earn their god's approval and occupy one of the fortresses. The number of convocations is in constant flux, though it is never fewer than nine and is always a multiple of that sacred number.

Within the Realm of Chaos, Tzeentch's daemons battle those of the other Dark Gods, staving off invasions or seeking to claim territory. Alliances are forged, broken and forged again, yet none can weave in or out of such treaties with as much skill as the minions of the Great Schemer. Tzeentch covets the Mortal Realms, and his forces actively pursue hundreds of different plots, such as shifting the strands of fate or covertly persuading mortal recruits to serve in Arcanite Cults. Like their patron, the convocations seek sources of magic, spread anarchy and corrupt ambitions. When illusion or manipulation fail, however, they resort to more direct methods, setting battlefields alight with volleys of spells and sheets of warpfire.

*Infinite forms there twist and churn, competing to claim the mind,
Trespassers there had better beware; the fate of fools is unkind.*

DOMAINS OF THE CULTS

Tzeentchian cults can be found in every realm save that of Azyr. They are master infiltrators, and through them the Scintillating Hosts have found their way into countless nations of man, aelf and duardin. In Chamon, they have worked a great conquest from which the lands, twisted beyond recognition, may never heal.

The Arcanites of Tzeentch work plans within plans to ensure their master's visions of strife come to pass. Few truly comprehend the magnitude or the complexity of these overlapping schemes, but they do their part, and that is enough. To a Magister or Summoner, the bringing of a cackling horde of daemons into reality might be the culmination of their life's work, but to the myriad plots of Tzeentch, they are but stitches in a greater tapestry.

Each conjuration and conquest is part of a wider skein of fate that binds the stuff of reality, imbues it with the energies of disorder, and brings it one step closer to becoming an annex of Tzeentch's Crystal Labyrinth. The lands of the Spiral Crux are a perfect illustration of this phenomenon. Though not even the canny Kharadron Overlords native to the Crux truly appreciate it, those regions most afflicted by Tzeentch's war have not been chosen at random.

Seen from the aetheric void, these profaned sites form the fire-and-orb symbol of Tzeentch, the Changer of the Ways. Griffon's Eyrie, the disastrous epicentre of the magical explosion caused by the death of a godbeast, forms the pulsating heart of the symbol. All those lands under its wider auspice have been renamed in Tzeentch's honour. Should the last few wholesome lands under the symbol fall to Tzeentch's faithful, the Spiral Crux will be forever his.

THE AZURE CROWN
A formation of floating isles replete with magical crystal glows at the Crux's heart.

THE SKY-PORTS ATTACK
Kharadron sky-fleets make ever more desperate forays into Tzeentchian territory.

AETHER WAR

One of the lesser known consequences of the necroquake was the scattering of the aether-gold sky-seams, which dictate the fortunes of the Kharadron sky-ports. Of late, there has been a mad rush to claim them once more. This has led profiteering duardin fleets to sail into the territory of the Tzeentchian cults at the heart of the Spiral Crux.

Barak-Nar's quest for riches saw the Kharadron Bjarnus Tragg utilise an aetheric forcefield to venture into the toxic skies controlled by the Cult of the Transient Form. Battle was joined above the clouds as Disc-riding Arcanites fought intrepid duardin for the bounty of the skies.

13

THE SPIRAL CRUX

Ocean of Scholars

Grungni's Fist · Site of Barak-Zon's first alliance with the Stormcast Eternals · Choking Throat · The Prism · Globule Island · Forgefire Fields · Brinetongue Bay · Lion's Hall · Impassable Peaks · Miner's Nirvana · Awhal Coast · Spinrikk's Forest · Onoglop Swamp · Ashpeaks · Mountains of Muspelzharr · Barrier Peaks · Rabble Coast · THE RUSTED WASTES · Knave Dwellings · Scryer's Tip · God's Hoard · The Steel Triplets · Ruins of the Golden Fortress · GAZAN ZHAR · Forest of Verdunst · Coast of Fine Barter · Aoga · Din · Ioth · Beryllium Sea · Barak-Zon · Andar · Mercurial Tower · Cloudring of Dharz · Patina Peaks · Stalia · Desolation of Urk · ARABLE HEARTHLANDS · Copperfang Peaks · The Dolmen Deeps · Coast of Thralls · Stratis Skull · Shoulderstrain Path · Eruption of Gralas · Nimblewood · Goldenspike · Dented Peaks · Bandit's Point · Ovus · Toolsman Awl · Skyscourge Volcanoes · The Stretch · The Godsclaw · Sea of Rituals · Webbed Kingdom · Drong Shipyards · The Bleakwoods · Domtanguan Mountains · Ruins of Prosperia · PROSPERIS · Drilltip Bay · Alchemist's Grave · Nonagon Isle · Cape Serpentine · Barak-Mhornar · Rivenlands · Charwood · Abyssal Canal · Breacher Bay · Blasphemer's Tip · Merchant's Mouth · Straits of Helsilver · Spike Coast · Ferrus Sea · Vale of Golden Idols · Twisted Horn · Galleon's Bane · The Bear · Flotilla Graveyard · Brass Mountains · Broken Kingdoms · Gleaming Sea · Inreach · VISCID FLUX · BEASTMAN VALE · Louper's Estuary · Granthium Mountains · Switchsoul Dais · Lake of Fuels · Tzaangrel Coast · Dontos Mountains · Lake Elixus · Vulcharc Peaks · Slitherspawn Wastes · Lake of Damned Duels · THE GREAT BEWILDERNESS · The Acid Pits · Crescent Peaks · Bay of Gilded Bones · Crystallised Cape · River Chilltan · Nineperil Coast · Drowning Leap · The Squid Coves · Tinker's Lee · Equus Spike

GRIFFON'S EYRIE

The heart of the Spiral Crux is a wasteland wracked with potent change-magic. To tarry there is to die.

THE SILVER TOWERS

The strongholds of the Gaunt Summoners have been spotted hovering over the Spiral Crux.

THE CHILDREN OF CHANGE

The daemons of Tzeentch are insanity and mayhem made manifest, the antithesis of order and law. In battle, they make for a maddening foe, chortling maniacally as they blast apart their enemies with dazzling spells and mimicking their agony as multicoloured flames burn away their victims' souls.

Tzeentchian daemons are physical manifestations of raw arcane energy, warped to reflect different aspects of their patron. As befits the Changer of the Ways, the nature of his minions varies greatly, although each is blessed with a portion of their master's strangeness and cunning. So infused are they with magic that the air about them takes on an unearthly glimmer. Likewise, their own colours and even material stability shift – sometimes they appear corporeal, other times bafflingly illusive.

As daemons, the Scintillating Hosts have need for neither nourishment nor rest, and they cannot be slain as can mortal creatures. It is possible to destroy a daemon's physical shell, but doing so only sends its spirit back to the Realm of Chaos, where it begins the painful process of reforming. The length of time this takes depends upon the daemon's size, strength and, most importantly, whether or not the being still carries their god's favour. In the case of the Horrors – that most numerous of all Tzeentchian daemons – even a solid,

killing blow is not nearly enough to end the threat. These creatures split into two lesser creatures before the eyes of their astonished adversaries – and should either of these be slain in turn, they will split again to form hideous creatures of spite and flame. Such impossibilities, so maddening to mortal onlookers, give Tzeentch a great deal of amusement.

It is difficult in the extreme for any one daemon to hold Tzeentch's attention for long; the god is not inclined to rouse from his introspections in order to concentrate on a single iteration of his immensity. So immersed is he in his weighty schemes that it has been many ages since Tzeentch's physical form left the Impossible Fortress at the heart of the Crystal Labyrinth. There, in the sanctum of the Hidden Library, the Great Conspirator prefers instead to read the infinite skeins of fate and to send forth his daemonic legions to advance his ineffable plans. The fates of individuals, be they mortal or daemonic, yield but the briefest flicker of interest or amusement before Tzeentch's attention moves elsewhere. Yet when taken together, the infinite complexities of every overlapping life, breaking soul and unintended consequence forms a mosaic of disaster that the god finds eternally enthralling.

In those areas rich in magic, the daemons of Tzeentch can manifest more easily. They thrive on the aetheric forces as a human thrives on clean air and water – without them, they cannot persist. Over the course of the Age of Chaos, the lands of the Mortal Realms, already rich in the stuff of magic as a result of their uncanny origins, became saturated with wild power. Since then, the daemons of Chaos have been able to take corporeal forms long enough to cause havoc everywhere they appear – sometimes even for years at a time, provided they keep to the places where eldritch energies can be drawn from the air to sustain their unnatural physiques. Should Tzeentch ever complete his dominion over the lands, the Realm of Chaos and the Mortal Realms would become one and the same, and his daemons would be able to exist there in perpetuity.

The onrush of the daemon legions of Tzeentch is a sight that can plunge the sane into raving madness. The very air shimmers with polychromatic colours as an outpouring of pure sorcery bursts above the oncoming masses. Capering Pink Horrors chortle as they advance, summoning mystic bolts from their strange fluted fingers as easily as an archer would draw an arrow from his quiver. Sullen Blue Horrors grumble behind, wreathed in azure fires, while bright yellow Brimstone Horrors dance around their feet. Like strange living mushrooms borne on clouds of superheated air, Flamers bound by, mutagenic fire pouring from their twisted limbs as they roar and screech from their many mouths. The skies, meanwhile, are streaked black in the wake of Burning Chariots, each a fiery comet of destruction that sends warpflame cascading into the ranks of the enemy to twist flesh and metal into horrendous new shapes. With them come airborne shoals of predatory Screamers that descend in stately, overlapping arcs to slash through the flesh of their prey with their bladed wings. Those who present a particularly delicious morsel of soul energy, perhaps because of their magical acumen or some supernatural strength from within, find themselves beset by dozens of these creatures at once, each frenzied with the need to clamp their toothy lamprey mouths upon the flesh of the gifted or the blessed.

The lesser of Tzeentch's daemons, the Horrors, are created as slaves and given little autonomy. It is their lot to follow orders given by those of higher rank, although even to these Tzeentch has bequeathed an unquenchable capricious streak. Other daemons, however, are granted far more self-reliance.

The Heralds are Tzeentch's lieutenants – though they may look little more than larger and more elaborate versions of Pink Horrors, they are blessed with cunning minds and devious ambition. On most occasions, it is they who lead the hordes. However, when the situation demands a true master of anarchy, one so steeped in the energies of Tzeentch that the air itself mutates and screams around it, a Lord of Change is dispatched to twist history to its master's whims.

The greater daemons known as Lords of Change are the most powerful of Tzeentch's immortal minions. These towering avian creatures are gifted near-total freedom to pursue Tzeentch's goals. It is they who set champions, Heralds and cults on their courses, and it is they who most often direct the legions in complex and ever-changing plans.

After Tzeentch issues commands to his armies, he contemplates their infinite effects. Gazing upon his creations with fascination, he is eager to watch his children plot, deceive and manipulate even their own forces in order to further their ambitions. Where things go awry, he drinks in the heady mix of improvisation and confusion – a rich loam from which moments of spontaneous genius can grow. When things go exactly according to plan, the Changer of the Ways taps his long talons together in a strange mixture of satisfaction and anxiety, for a predictable outcome courts boredom and there is nothing Tzeentch hates more. And so he avidly watches the unravelling of every strand of fate, each a small part of his Great Plan – though, in the end, all fates are woven into one, and the ultimate outcome is doom.

TO SHAPE THE INVISIBLE

The Changer of the Ways has little time for the cantrips and hedge magics of cowardly dabblers, instead rewarding those who gather vast concentrations of magical force and let them loose upon the world. In the time of the Arcanum Optimar, this effect has become even more pronounced. It is easier than ever for mages to summon magical familiars and seal dark pacts to increase their own power, or to conjure predatory spells and grand hexes that can cripple or destroy dozens of their adversaries in a matter of moments.

Some of these spells gain notoriety or fame amongst the Arcanites and will come easily to the Scintillating Hosts. These can see their mages attempt to prove their power over the ineffable by casting certain spells and invocations. Some wizards increase their arcane knowledge by conjuring a Tome of Eyes – a semi-real, outsize grimoire that appears on a pillar of magical flame. As the would-be scholar reads the forbidden spells from its burning pages, they are read in turn by the evil-looking orbs that stare out from it, their soul scrutinised and their secrets taken for later use. Others summon a Burning Sigil of Tzeentch – after years of keeping their allegiance secret, they revel in displaying their icon of their true patron. The sheer mutative power of this change-sigil will see all those around it horrifically mutated and twisted by Chaos, though not always to their detriment. Only the bravest mages dare to summon a Daemonic Simulacrum, the swirling magic they conjure taking form as the evil, avian heads of Lords of Change. These can tear the minds from the bodies of those nearby, leaving only drooling imbeciles. Woe betide the caster who stands too close, for the mind of a mage is the most delicious of all…

THE SCINTILLATING HOSTS

To mortal eyes, the kaleidoscopic daemon hosts of Tzeentch are impossible to distinguish from one another before the beholder is slain or driven to insanity. There is method to the madness, however. Though none save perhaps the Architect of Fate himself can follow all the ever-changing configurations, they all abide by his strange laws.

Tzeentch's forces are many and varied, their compositions often in flux. This fluid organisation, quite the opposite of Khorne's militant and hierarchical cohorts or the cyclical formations that serve Nurgle, delights their patron. Yet there remain hidden strictures that please Tzeentch, foremost amongst them the sacred number nine. Each convocation is led by a mighty Lord of Change and is divided into nine hosts. Each of these is led in turn by a subordinate greater daemon, Herald or other powerful minion. The convocation's master may occasionally commandeer one of its hosts itself, should such a course of action appear propitious.

All of Tzeentch's daemons are dedicated to furthering their patron's rule – indeed, as part of his essence, they rarely do anything else – but as they go about their tasks, they incline towards particular methods depending on the convocation to which they belong. The daemons of the Grand Cabal, for instance, represent Tzeentch in his role as the Great Conspirator, preferring espionage, intrigue, politics and clandestine sorcery to achieve their aims. They are perhaps the least openly warlike of the Scintillating Hosts and favour winning their battles in the landscape of the mind rather than in the open field.

The Hosts Duplicitous share a taste for misdirection – though, for them, it is an end unto itself. When forced to engage in person, they swathe themselves in mirages and shimmering illusions. Combined with the Horrors' innate ability to split, reform into new bodies and split again, this makes them an amorphous and bewildering foe to face upon the field of battle. No simple sword blade can strike true against the Hosts Duplicitous; to win a victory against them, the weapons of the mind must prevail.

The Hosts Arcanum were amongst the first to invade Aqshy's Great Parch and still have a great presence there to this day. Ranging from parasitic familiars that suckle upon their unwitting masters, hiding their true forms, to towering greater daemons that cackle maniacally as they devour magical artefacts and spell-wrought tomes, the Hosts Arcanum have a myriad forms. Screamers are common in their number, attracted to the invisible haze of energy that gathers around magic users as sea-feeders are attracted to plankton in the ocean.

The Hosts Arcanum have long sought to claim the bounty of the Agloraxi Empire. Indeed, it was they who led those proud mages to the brink of utter annihilation, stoking their pride and supplying ever more arcane trinkets, mysteries and riddles to unlock. It was this same overweening hubris that saw the Agloraxi take to the skies upon their giant floating city and, in doing so, offend Khorne enough that the Blood God struck their metropolis from the heavens, causing it to shatter into a million pieces across the Flamescar Plateau – much to the amusement of their hidden 'benefactor', Tzeentch.

The Transcendental Change are birds of a different feather, relying heavily upon the power of mutation. They use transformational magics to cause immediate and traumatic physical alteration to their foes, the environment – even themselves.

Although any of Tzeentch's daemons can appear in all of the different convocations, some show a proclivity for specific ones. For instance, Flamers always feature prominently in the hosts of the Eternal Conflagration, while the mind-melting anarchy of the Unbound Flux typically revolves around cavorting masses of Horrors. These hosts are more given to open war, for they rejoice in the colour, noise and light of their master's power unleashed in its most vibrant and destructive form.

Each of the convocations strives to garner the lion's share of their master's praise. For a daemon to earn its master's favour is to live and prosper; should it instead displease its lord, it may be banished, diminished or even subsumed to forfeit its sentience altogether. As one would expect from the minions of Tzeentch, there is no end to their machinations as they push their own agendas and sabotage those of their rivals. When the Great Schemer weighs the tributes paid to him and proclaims his judgement, the sigils of each convocation writhe upon the Shifting Pyramid of Yrch deep in the Crystal Labyrinth, blazing into a new hierarchical order.

The nine most favoured Scintillating Hosts are each granted control of one of the Fractal Fortresses, and their fallen are resurrected more quickly from the Nine Gates. Not surprisingly, this new order can turn quickly – it is as fickle as Tzeentch himself. Even his most favoured and trusted daemons walk a tightrope of causality that can see them rise to new heights or plummet into the darkness of disgrace. One need only listen to the legend of the Lord of Change known as Kairos Fateweaver, hurled deep into the Well of Eternity to sate Tzeentch's curiosity, in order to appreciate how capricious the Changer of the Ways truly is.

THE FLESH ASCENDED

Not all daemons begin their existence as such. El'an'zeth, the Ninefold Promise, was once a mortal servant of the Great Schemer, granted the gift of daemonhood after a lifetime spent gathering forbidden knowledge and lost secrets. He now stands eternal guard over the library-city of Uzalith.

Those who worship Tzeentch do so for power, knowledge and immortality. Many find their way into Arcanite Cults, wherein secrets must be unlocked and trials passed to ascend through the hierarchy. So it was for El'an'zeth, the Ninefold Promise, whose mortal name was Elias the Seer. Naturally gifted in the arts of sorcery, but also keenly intellectual and mercilessly acquisitive in his quest for knowledge, Elias spent much of his life as a hermit in the wilderness. His only vice was to meddle in the fates of man, duardin and aelf from afar, taking joy in each manipulation.

This tendency led Elias down a dark path. He angered the scions of Khorne when he sent false omens to the Skullfiend Tribe, leading them into the desiccating wilderness of the Arid Swathe. When the Bloodbound warlord learned the cause of the error, Elias fled across the Mortal Realms, joining a cell of the Guild of Summoners within the winding volcanic caverns of Vindicarum. Living in fear, he turned to the one god who claimed he could protect him – almighty Tzeentch. He made many sacrifices to his new patron and earned ever more arcane prizes as he climbed through the ranks.

At first, Elias avoided the pitfalls of pride and avarice that would have blasted the minds of lesser souls, prioritising those plots of Tzeentch that benefited mankind over the other mortal races. He even navigated the warped corridors of a Silver Tower when he was finally called to account for himself, returning with boons of esoteric wisdom and mutation that seemed beneficial at first but ultimately paved his way to daemonhood. So is the path to glory travelled by those with the strength and willpower to do so, for much is gifted to those who dedicate themselves wholly to Tzeentch.

NINE SHALL BE THEIR NUMBER

Each of the convocations that gather in Tzeentch's name has its own symbol. Only nine such icons can occupy the prime positions upon their patron's Shifting Pyramid of Yrch, where the fates burn hot. Those currently favoured by Tzeentch have held their status since the beginning of the Age of Sigmar, but – as ever – change is inevitable…

THE ETERNAL CONFLAGRATION

Blazing with the unnatural fires of change are these lords of wyrdflame. Daemons all, their eyes are embers of malevolence, their blades the tongues of mutative infernos set loose to wreak havoc on the flesh of their foes. All that are kissed by these fires find their mortal bodies transmogrified into surreal forms, screaming in their last moments as writhing tentacled blobs, statues of bone or frozen crystal glimmering for the glory of Tzeentch.

To face the Eternal Conflagration in battle is to gape at a kaleidoscopic display of power – and, should the viewer not see sense enough to flee, to be consumed by those same daemonic fires. Their icon is the burning triskele, an ever-turning wheel that hurls out pure change. Of all Tzeentch's hosts, these are the least subtle, and their rivals often scoff at the uncomplicated approach to victory taken by their master, the Radiant Lord: let the fires of change run wild, and almighty Tzeentch will do the rest. Yet in this purity of focus, they find great favour with the Changer of the Ways. It pleases Tzeentch to see the mortal clay of his foes rendered fluid and turned against its owners. In the bedazzling brightness of the Eternal Conflagration's assault, a small measure of his anarchic and ever-changing will is made manifest.

THE HOSTS DUPLICITOUS

Ask them no questions, lest they deign to answer. Nine times nine are the distorted truths that they shall tell, and madness will be their only reply. Illusion dances about the daemons of the Hosts Duplicitous, for they hold the power of deceit as sacred above all, never revealing their true intent to anyone. Even their symbol is a contradiction, with two screaming daemon faces gainsaying each other despite being a single entity. Such is this convocation's all-consuming need to tear down truth and displace justice with disorder that they will go to great lengths to confound and undermine the cities and metropolises of the Mortal Realms. This can be done through dissembling whispers, secret rituals and obfuscatory vandalism, but when the time of the daemon waxes nigh, it is achieved through large-scale invasions. With their master, the Phantom Lord, at their head, the notion of abiding stability and order is proven to be the greatest lie of all.

THE HOSTS ARCANUM

From the great libraries of the Impossible Fortress they hail, thoughts burning with forbidden secrets. Purest sorcery is their propensity, for they are the arch-spellcasters of all reality. No incantation is beyond their reach, no mystery impenetrable to their piercing gaze. Those who seek skill in the arts of sorcery will sometimes make offerings to this convocation, as they are more proficient in the ways of magic than any other daemons. They are all too happy to grant esoteric power to such supplicants; by bringing chaotic magic to the realms, they can peer into the works of men and weaken the division between the Mortal Realms and their home domain. Their icon, the all-seeing eye, hints at this desire to witness every act of sorcery there is.

It is the Hosts Arcanum that the Blue Scribes fight alongside most frequently, for the lords and Heralds of this daemon army amass eldritch lore as a stone gathers moss, and even other daemons can learn from them. Like attracts like, and the more mastery the Hosts Arcanum show over their strange arts, the more they find the energies of the realms falling under their power.

THE TRANSCENDENTAL CHANGE

None are as perpetually in flux as the Transcendental Change, for they are the true children of the Great Mutator. They embody the power of alteration, unleashing wave upon wave of irresistible change such that their enemies, their own warriors and even the battlefield itself are distorted and remade in the multifarious aspects of almighty Tzeentch. In this lack of discernment is a strange kind of power – it is not for nothing that they claim to be the closest in nature to the elemental core of the Changer of the Ways.

THE GRAND CABAL

With infinite care, they wield intrigue and espionage as others wield blades. The Grand Cabal seek out those who covet power or those who guard it with jealousy and fear. These they manipulate, fanning the flames of paranoia and avarice until an inferno of strife erupts. It is the joy of the Grand Cabal to infiltrate the strongholds of the mortal races – several of the Cities of Sigmar are being slowly strangled by their interweaving plots and schemes. Though the Order of Azyr attempts to unpick these webs, they have been outwitted a hundred times over.

SEEKERS OF INFINITE WISDOM

The locks break and fall away, one by one. Stolen keys turn in forbidden doorways as runes of warding flare and die like the death of distant stars. No barrier can turn them aside, and no warning shall they heed, for the Seekers of Infinite Wisdom will dare any consequence in their quest for omniscience. They seek to unpick the riddles of the cosmos, amongst them the mysteries of the Realmgates and the aetheric void. These daemons gladly delve into secrets best left alone. Fear them, for what they know can kill…

LEGION OF FATE

It is they who read the weaving streams of time eternal, twisting chance and pruning potential even as they redirect the paths of those whose deeds threaten their agendas. All knowledge spreads before their countless eyes like an impossible vista, and matters temporal are as inconsequential zephyrs to them. Much like their idol Kairos, for the Legion of Fate, the stuff of causality is as a ball of yarn to a cat. They love nothing more than to cut away the skeins of destiny and so damn mortal endeavours to ruination.

LORDS OF DOMINION

Countless are those who dance unknowingly to the pandemoniac musics of the Lords of Dominion. It is their talons that grip the puppets' strings, their scripts from which the hapless unwittingly read. Many do their bidding, though few know it, for here are the mind-thieves and the suborners of will. Supreme manipulation is their province. They do this not to further some dramatic endgame, nor do the civil wars they bring about fulfil a greater purpose – they pull the strings purely for the thrill of mastery over others.

THE UNBOUND FLUX

Spreaders of anarchy and slayers of reason, the Unbound Flux bring into reality those horrors that should remain forever trammelled within the minds of the deranged. Mental strength melts like hot wax beneath their unravelling gaze and ordered thought deforms into mayhem. Stern minds and staunch hearts run mad at their touch, for the Unbound Flux bring change in such purity that no armour can be proof against it. To look upon their works is to go insane; madness is both their weapon and their legacy to the Mortal Realms.

TZEENTCH ARCANITES

Tzeentch does not rely on his daemon armies alone to conquer the Eight Realms; the Changer of the Ways has lured many mortal followers to his inscrutable cause. The Arcanites and their growing cults play a crucial role in the Great Schemer's plots of conquest.

Like his brothers, Tzeentch has corrupted countless mortal servants. Once, they belonged to tribes of men, but they became ensnared, lured by promises of power, glory, forbidden lore and immortality. Great champions rose, gathering those that followed the dark paths into armies, and during the Age of Chaos, their conquests spread across the Mortal Realms, furthering Tzeentch's ineffable plans. Yet those Slaves to Darkness were not enough to satisfy the Changer of the Ways. In his infinite cunning, Tzeentch created other types of mortal armies, more devious and gifted in magic than any that had come before.

Whether veiled by illusionary magics or hidden as part of a clandestine society, the Arcanites have grown in power and number. Although some of these hidden cults and secretive armies have existed for generations, only recently have they begun to make their nefarious presence felt in the Mortal Realms. Some made their lairs in secret forest clearings or places rich in eldritch energies; others were secreted right under the noses of the forces of Order. As Sigmar's new cities grew, so too did the Arcanites, spreading like some hidden malignancy.

Although typically covert in nature, the Arcanites strike when the time is right, unleashing a bombardment of sorcerous destruction. Kairic Acolytes, their faces obscured by cryptic masks, chant sizzling arcane bolts into existence that arc into their foes. Sects of Kairic Acolytes are secretive, with many continuing to grow undetected in human tribes and cities across the Mortal Realms. To maintain their secrecy, the more conspicuous aspects of their altered forms are concealed beneath illusions and sorcerous obfuscations. The Acolytes are careful to remove their idealised disguises out of sight of even their fellow cultists, so that none know the true identities of

the other members. Great pains are taken to arrange meetings in hidden locations, where the Kairic Acolytes learn the secrets of magic from a Kairic Adept or Magister in the cult's cabal. Acolytes all aspire to become powerful wizards, supremely confident that it will be they who master Chaos and never the other way around. Each level of advancement brings new secrets. Acolytes who show promise are granted boons, such as occult grimoires, talismans from the Crystal Labyrinth to boost arcane abilities – even Vulcharcs, carrion birds so corrupted by Chaos that they hunt and feast upon magic.

All Tzeentch's Arcanite agents are tasked with manipulating events to turn destiny in their god's favour. An alchemist might conduct disturbing research with dark magic, while a worker gang might plot to burn down a nearby district, pinning the blame on the different races that live amongst the Cities of Sigmar. Feuds are begun and political alliances torn asunder. Insidiously, Chaos spreads. When the cabal of an Arcanite Cult feels it is time, they gather together, cast off their illusions and strike. Kairic Acolytes pool their energies in order to barrage their foe with sorcerous bolts; when close-quarters combat nears, they close in with murderous intent, chanting all the while. Any foes that survive their magical assault must then face the Acolytes' blades, along with those of their Tzaangor allies.

The leaders of the Arcanite Cults take a dizzying variety of forms. The Tzaangors are avian beastmen who serve Tzeentch, their unnatural instincts and animal savagery augmented with a keen, if cruel, intelligence. The Tzaangor elites – the Enlightened and the Skyfires – ride the air atop scintillating Discs of Tzeentch, sometimes accompanied to war by hulking Ogroid Thaumaturges. These brutes hurl roiling fireblasts, from which spring Horrors, before lowering their mighty horns to charge the foe.

Magisters are master sorcerers who blast the enemy into swirling motes of multicoloured light or transmute them into crystal. Crackling shields of magical power spark and flare as enemy blades and bolts rebound harmlessly against their incantations. Fatemasters are cunning warriors surrounded by an aura that alters destiny in their favour, while Tzaangor Shamans ride upon daemonic Discs and cause the air to boil with mutagenic spells, each transforming foes into mockeries of their former selves.

After battle, the Arcanite Cults fade back into the hinterlands, covering their tracks with illusions or assuming false guises to live undetected amongst unsuspecting populations. Once returned to obscurity, the cults recommence their secret plots. In the wilds, fell flux-cairns are raised, while in settlements, feuds are ignited and illicit political alliances forged. Foul rituals summon daemons, dark rites pinpoint the locations of arcane artefacts and events are manipulated to twist fate in Tzeentch's favour. The Arcanite Cults constantly grow, luring in further conspirators, beguiling the power-hungry and corrupting newcomers. As it spreads its influence, each cult awaits its next god-given task. It will not be long in coming, for Tzeentch has many plans, and change is inevitable…

EXCELSIS FALLING

Excelsis was once a jewel in Sigmar's empire, a port city on Ghur's Coast of Tusks. Built around a bay that surrounded the colossal pillar of sigmarite known as the Spear of Mallus, it was one of the new metropolises that swiftly grew to glory after the Stormcast Eternals won beachheads across the Mortal Realms. The city had thrived on harnessing, refining and monetising splinters and shards of the Spear of Mallus, for that mighty edifice had descended from the heavens of Azyr and was rich in the energies of prophecy. Those who absorbed the glimpses of the future afforded to them by each 'glimmering' experienced flashes of precognitive vision that could lead them to further riches. Excelsis became a centre of trade, amassing a vast naval force and powerful allies in the form of the Scourge Privateers who magically subdued the monsters of the ocean.

But the city's heavens-sent boon cast a long shadow. Tzeentch coveted the prophetic powers flowing through the pillar of sigmarite and wished to harness them for himself – the Spear of Mallus had been cast from the heavens and, with the right enchantments, might be used to reach them once more. If nothing else, to unlock the secrets of the magical metal would be a valuable prize. In furtherance of their god's desires, the Cult of the Fated Path infiltrated each strata of society, from common scribes to vaunted aristocrats. They were led by a sinister masked Magister known as Ortam Vermyre, who had

worked his way up to the position of High Arbiter but, in secret, counted many daemons amongst his allies. Slowly, painstakingly, he established a web of influence across the city. So careful was he that even the Knights Excelsior – whose Stormkeep, the Consecralium, towered over the city – knew not of his agenda. Though they marched through the streets each day on their way to war, and though they were known for their pitiless purging of all things tainted by Chaos, the Stormcast Eternals were preoccupied with the ongoing battle against the orruk tribes of the surrounding foothills and the vast part of their strength was out in the field. If not for the intervention of a common Freeguild sergeant, who stumbled across evidence of the fate in store for the city, the secret plot to raze Excelsis would have come to fruition all but unopposed. But that was not to be.

When the skies tore upon to send hosts of daemons spilling into reality, much of the noble quarter was destroyed, but the defenders had been given enough time to marshal a solid counter-attack and stop the city being consumed entirely by warpfire. For many years to come, the city's protectors turned their gaze inwards, yet in neglecting their purges of the orruks in the hills, they courted another kind of disaster. Blessed strife and unbound change would come to Excelsis once more, and, one way or another, Tzeentch's goal of seeing the city consumed by disaster would be fulfilled soon enough…

THE ARCH-CONSPIRATORS

At the dark heart of an Arcanite Cult, there will always be a sorcerer. They are the founder of the cult, the leader of a hidden army and the interpreter of Tzeentch's divine will. Forming a cabal around themselves, the leader grows their cult through a web of agents, slowly amassing a secret army to strike in the name of the Changer of the Ways.

By the light of a stolen candle, a scribe pores over dusty books, seeking reward for his research and desperate for answers to his many questions. What would an individual sacrifice to possess arcane knowledge? How far would one debase oneself to unlock a secret hidden for untold ages?

Hypnotised by the lure of forbidden knowledge or even a simple desire to learn, many of the brightest minds of the Mortal Realms are led astray, lured onwards down the path of damnation in a quest for enlightenment. One carefully uncovered secret leads to another until, in slow increments, a soul has bartered away far more than they ever meant to. There can be no turning back, for those touched by the faintest trace of Chaos would do anything to avoid being hunted down and dragged into the open by the agents of Sigmar. The witch-hunting Order of Azyr are not above torture, and the Stormcast Eternals practise rough and deadly justice. By exploiting this fear, preying upon those who are most zealous in their search for arcana, do the Tzeentchian cults recruit.

Each Arcanite Cult is built around a sorcerer who is favoured by the Changer of the Ways – for a time, at least. Driven by Tzeentch's unknowable will, a Magister, Tzaangor Shaman or Fatemaster lays the foundations, taking on apprentices worthy of their magical teachings and seeking others that can be taught.

So it was with Tri'chlan, the founder of the Cult Esoteric, a secret order dedicated to plumbing the depths of the most forbidden eldritch arts in Hammerhal Ghyra. Tri'chlan had long ago sold his soul to Tzeentch in exchange for vast knowledge and, in doing so, had become a Magister – a sorcerer granted mutations as well as dark gifts. Concealing his fall to Chaos with powerful illusions, Tri'chlan maintained his position within the learned halls of the Grand Academy, a temple of enlightenment in the lush garden district of Hammerhal Ghyra. There, he sought those who, like himself, were questing for hidden knowledge, frustrated by the foolish barriers put in place by the Collegiate Arcane and the Eldritch Council that forbade the study or use of Chaos energies.

Most aspirants were rejected – they lacked the proper conviction or their abilities were not advanced enough. Those who passed were anointed as Kairic Acolytes, and their true training began. Rite after rite, sacrifice after sacrifice took place. At first, all that was required of the aspirants was their complicity as they watched horrendous acts of blasphemy and daemon-worship in the cellars and basements of the cult's strongholds in Hammerhal Ghyra. Then, the aspirants were required to sacrifice captive Dryads and forest spirits taken from the blight-weakened woods of Verdia. When the act of killing in the name of Tzeentch became second nature to them, human sacrifice was introduced, and the damnation of the aspirants was finally sealed. So did the Cult Esoteric grow powerful indeed, as a hundred cults had done before it.

It is a rare cult that boasts only a single sorcerer, for its commander typically forms a cabal – a small inner circle of leaders, all of whom are masters of sorcery. New cultists must be recruited and trained, and those who pass ritual testing

must be formed into covens. All the cultists and any meeting sites must be hidden from detection through illusion, misdirection and assassination. Secrecy is at the heart of the cabal and a great portion of the leaders' magical powers are directed towards concealing their cult's growing numbers. In this way, many cults have been seeded across the Mortal Realms, with only Tzeentch knowing the exact number and location of them all.

As cults become larger, they risk exposing their covert nature, and so metamorphosis becomes necessary. Upon filling its cabal and covens to a multiple of nine, a cult will split and its members will branch out – just as Tri'chlan's order sowed the seeds of the mutation-worshipping Cult of Blessed Transition. Such is the way of ambition, and such is the way of Tzeentch. Indeed, it is only the ambitious who willingly seek entry into one of these hidden societies, eager to learn secrets, rise from Acolyte to Adept, join the inner cabal and, finally, lead a cult themselves. Each new stage of a cultist's advancement unlocks further lore, which they voraciously absorb. As they do so, all coven members compete for their leaders' praise, just as the cabal seeks dark blessings from even higher powers, calling upon either Lords of Change or upon almighty Tzeentch himself.

SECRETS OF THE CULTS

Arcanite Cults are secretive, clandestine organisations hidden by illusion and deceit. Although they are dedicated to change and the downfall of Order, there is some method to the madness that binds together each cult. At the head there is always a cabal, and underneath them is a group of three or more covens that do their bidding.

Each fully-fledged Arcanite Cult is a major assemblage of mortal Tzeentch worshippers, ranging from factions of ninety-nine souls to vast organisations numbering in the thousands. Each cult is led by a small but powerful group of warrior-sorcerers known as a cabal, and it may have further allies in the form of henchmen and honoured guests.

Every one of the Arcanite Cults is utterly dedicated to fulfilling the aims of their deity, but like the convocations of Tzeentch's daemons, each cult does so by favouring one of their god's many aspects. Those who flock to the banners of the Cult of Oracles are steeped in precognitive omens, portents and prophecies; their actions, intrigues and wars are all based around the predictive nature of their future sight. The Cult of the Transient Form, however, favours mutations and change-magics to achieve their ends, while the Cult of a Thousand Eyes prefers to work behind a veil of secrecy, casting spells of manipulation and control. Naturally, the great cults each regard themselves as superior to their brethren and strive to maintain ascendancy. Open warfare between the cults is rare but not unheard of, and betrayals and power struggles are frequent indeed.

An Arcanite Cult usually contains three to nine covens. Covens are distinct groups of devotees made up, in turn, of three separate groups known as sects. When a cult numbers a multiple of nine covens, it will keep to the sacred number by splitting apart, just as a Horror divides or a globular aetherfish splits upon glutting itself on the raw magic of Tzeentch's realm. The extraneous covens then take on a new identity and name. These 'splinter cults' will often share the same colourations of armour and aspects of iconography as their parent cult, and they will fight alongside them with only scant thoughts of treachery.

Many important cult rituals are carried out not by the cabal but by its lieutenants and subordinates. Some of these henchmen are exclusively allied with certain cults, but others can be found across the spectrum. Perhaps the most commonly seen lieutenant is the Curseling, also known as an Eye of Tzeentch. This is a wizard whose body is host to a Tretchlet – a minor daemon that grafts onto or sprouts from its bearer, conferring strange gifts and whispering counsel. The Tretchlet's ability to detect lies and glean a person's innermost secrets make Curselings excellent in their role

of testing aspirants to the cult. The souls of those deemed unworthy are fed to the sinister Tretchlet, thereby creating symbiosis between sorcerer and spirit. Stranger still are the Ogroid Thaumaturges, hulking beings that blaze from within with supernatural flame. Little is known of these mysterious brutes, but they are steeped in dark lore and their command of the flames of Tzeentch is second to none. Within Arcanite Cults, the Ogroid Thaumaturges bear titles like Thaumapriest or Master of Faneflame, for they lead the rituals that call upon warpfire and teach its secrets to the Kairic Acolytes.

Other types of lieutenant exist, such as the Totemshriekers and Prophet-horns. It is also not unusual for Arcanite Cults to summon aid from the Realm of Chaos or even enlist the help of a Daemon Prince – although who controls whom is not always clear.

Occasionally, one of the Gaunt Summoners may assume command of an Arcanite Cult – or perhaps merely join it for a time to serve his own nefarious purposes. As there are but nine of these terrifyingly powerful beings in existence, they are greatly revered by all of Tzeentch's cultists.

LORDS OF THE SILVER TOWERS

The Gaunt Summoners are the most trusted mortal servants of the Change God, nine wizards of formidable power charged with furthering Tzeentch's intricately woven plans. Each claims dominion over one of the Silver Towers, fortresses of crystal and magic that appear across the Mortal Realms seemingly at random, always leaving madness in their wake. Such are the sorcerous gifts bestowed upon the Gaunt Summoners that they can twist the very landscape beneath them into unnatural shapes, immolate entire armies with burning witchfire, or transmute their foes into bubbling pools of protean matter. Despite their allegiance to Tzeentch, the Gaunt Summoners currently chafe under the domination of Archaon the Everchosen, the mortal champion of the Dark Gods, who sought out the sorcerers' true names at great cost and, in doing so, found a way to bind them to his service. Archaon utilises their talents of prophecy and illusion to aid his grand conquest of the realms – a situation Tzeentch seems content to allow, for the time being at least. The Gaunt Summoners themselves long for the day when they can escape from the Everchosen's iron grasp.

THE HIDDEN ORDER

An Arcanite Cult typically comprises three to nine covens, each of which is made up of three sects. The cult is led by an inner circle of powerful sorcerers called a cabal, who may delegate power to henchmen such as Curselings and Ogroid Thaumaturges. Gaunt Summoners that deign to assist a cult are referred to as 'honoured guests'. The exact structure of a cult is in constant flux, but the basic elements are common to all.

ARCANITE CABAL

- Magisters
- Tzaangor Shamans
- Fatemasters

HENCHMEN

- Curselings
- Ogroid Thaumaturges

HONOURED GUESTS

- Gaunt Summoners

The ruling cabal may ally with independent agents and temporary allies if it will further their arcane goals.

The cult's cabal may be formed of Magisters, Tzaangor Shamans and Fatemasters, though overall authority usually falls to but one of these powerful individuals.

The Gaunt Summoners that align themselves to the Arcanite Cults are held in both fear and awe by the initiated.

WITCHFYRE COVEN (3 SECTS)

 Kairic Acolytes

 Kairic Acolytes

 Tzaangor Enlightened

Witchfyre Covens are formed of Kairic Acolytes who demonstrate an aptitude for conjuring the fires of change, together with a Tzaangor Enlightened escort.

ALTER-KIN COVEN (3 SECTS)

 Kairic Acolytes

 Tzaangors

 Tzaangor Skyfires

Alter-kin Covens are masters of mutating magic. To stand within the aura of change that surrounds them is to risk an agonising transformation.

SKYSHOAL COVEN (3 SECTS)

 Tzaangor Skyfires

 Tzaangor Skyfires

 Tzaangor Enlightened

Tzaangors that form covens with Enlightened and Skyfires fight with heightened ferocity, eager to prove themselves before their elevated kin.

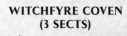

THE MARKS OF CHANGE

When the Arcanites go to war, eldritch symbols that were once concealed under voluminous robes are displayed for all to see. Whether emblazoned on artefacts, shimmering on standards and banners or tattooed on their skin, those who have tired of keeping their allegiance hidden now wish to show their true colours to the world.

The Arcanites of the Cult Cognita bear tomes inscribed with their sacred mark and penned in the blood of witches. They are said to know the truth behind Slaanesh's fall, though they keep silent on the matter.

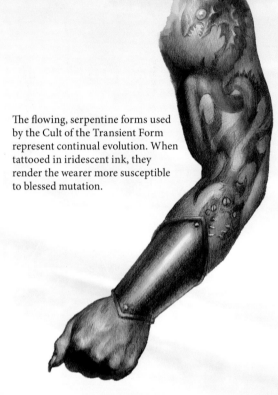

The flowing, serpentine forms used by the Cult of the Transient Form represent continual evolution. When tattooed in iridescent ink, they render the wearer more susceptible to blessed mutation.

The scrying orb is the sigil of the Cult of Oracles, they who seek to disrupt the natural order of the stars. Gifted in the arts of prophecy, they fear only the Seraphon, who protect the celestial world at all costs.

Wisps of flame circling an all-seeing eye is the sigil of the wyrdfire-obsessed Pyrofane Cult. To the untutored eye, it appears as a simple gold disc; only under the scrutiny of a cultist does the icon show its true form.

The Eye Entwined – often worn as a living, glaring eyeball incorporated into stylised jewellery – is the sign of the Cult of Twisted Fate. Revelling in cruel ironies wrought on a grand scale, their patrons drink in the final denouements of their treacherous plans.

27

The banners of the Guild of Summoners are daubed in the vile by-products of the Horrors slain and reborn in their service.

The Cult Pandemonius reveres the 'daemon's bite', thinking it the truest incarnation of Tzeentch's will. Their icon is a ravening, avian maw, the change that consumes all.

A crescent replete with staring eyeballs is the hallmark of the Cult of a Thousand Eyes. Their many spies and agents are scattered across the cities of the realms.

The Eldritch Cult make it their business to recruit from the ambitious and often frustrated novices of the Collegiate Arcane. Those inducted soon find Tzeentch's mark is upon them.

SKEINS OF FATE AFLAME

The infinitely complex weave of fate, barely glimpsed by even the most gifted mortal seer, is the plaything of almighty Tzeentch. His disciples have striven to tear it, rework it and set it ablaze in a thousand different ways, some of which have resonated across the centuries as works of dark genius.

● THE AGE OF MYTH ●

THE WHISPERING TOMES

Tzeentch's presence in the Mortal Realms starts as little more than a web of suspicions and vague memories of treacherous entities lurking in the darkness. However, when the rising nations of Sigmar's first civilisations lay down their knowledge in the form of the written word, Tzeentch finds a way in. Through the waking dreams of overworked scribes half-asleep at their calligrapher's lecterns, his daemon whisperers introduce words that have no right to be in the language of mortals. Slowly, syllable by syllable, the Dark Tongue infiltrates the most esoteric of tomes – and as those grimoires whisper softly in the night, the notion of pacts with entities from beyond the Mortal Realms is introduced to the minds of ambitious men.

GLOSSOLALIA IN THE DARK TONGUE

The research of obscure languages becomes highly fashionable among the scholastic brotherhoods of Hysh. The words of the Dark Tongue, having permeated not only the books of learned men but also the automatic speech of corrupted shamans, are spoken out loud for the thrill of it – the fact that those who do so often end up bleeding from the mouth only adds to its illicit appeal.

In the depths of the Nasroan Catacombs, a cabal of scholars take their experiments to the next level, hoping to unlock a secret source of power. Their chanting escalates out of control until they are speaking in tongues; in doing so, they thin reality, and the unclean light that streams out from the Realm of Chaos infects them with the will of Tzeentch. Silently they leave, each heading for a different Realmgate so that they might babble their unclean truths to a hundred unsullied nations.

STAINED GLASS

In the glass galleries and atriums of the Ninespire, the name of the greater daemon Kairos Fateweaver is said aloud for the first time in the Mortal Realms. The colourful lead-lined windows of that ancient and cosmopolitan city flicker and move, triumphal scenes and coronations being replaced by renditions of terrible massacres and burning cities. It is the cause of great wonderment, but, thus far, the city's existence has been so untroubled by strife that it causes little more than ripples of unease. Such is the complacency of the people of Ninespire that none realise the scenes foretell the events of the age to come. Over the course of the next few centuries, Kairos Fateweaver takes great pleasure in ensuring every one of the hellish scenes comes to pass.

● THE AGE OF CHAOS ●

TRANSCENDENT TREACHERY

In Chamon, the godbeast known as the lode-griffon settles in the heart of the Spiral Crux. The land is reshaped by the metallurgical apocalypse that results, and when the beast is finally slain, its death scream splits reality to let Tzeentch's daemons pour through. Soon after, the beastmen of that region raise their Herdstones across the Great Bewilderness. Runcor Hagbitten kills everything in his path that bears man-scent or values civilisation. Even the illusions of the Tzeentch Arcanites cannot save them, as the Transcendental Change discover to their cost during the massacre of the Vulcharc Peaks.

By the light of a twisted moon, the spellcaster known as Mater Muta turns herself and her followers into Tzaangors. The Allherd track them down, but now that they bear the scent of beastmen, they are not slain; instead, they are subsumed into the Allherd.

Over the coming months, the outlying elements of Hagbitten's Allherd number more and more blue-skinned, beaked mutants who pay obeisance to Tzeentch and fewer of the original gor-kin. Only when the Tzaangors outnumber the other beastmen two to one does Mater Muta reveal the truth – that the hunt is futile, and that she has been slowly changing the beastmen that once pursued her into fresh acolytes for Tzeentch. Outraged, Hagbitten himself lowers his horns and charges Mater Muta, only to be turned into a Chaos Spawn the moment his horn-tip grazes her flank. Muta's Tzaangors overthrow the Hagbitten horde, and the Great Bewilderness is claimed in Tzeentch's name.

THE AETHER-EATERS OF THE GREAT PARCH

Intending to cleanse the Agloraxi homelands of Tzeentchian influence, the magocracy of the Great Parch cast a vast pyroclastic spell – the same rite that once ignited the Kindling Forest. However, the Blue Scribes that are ransacking the Agloraxi's shattered citadels in search of new spells to hoard have learnt well of the mages' power. They conduct the numberless shoals of Screamers and Burning Chariots that follow in their wake to corral and consume the raging fires as they cascade across Aspiria. Even as the magical flames of Aqshy billow across the landscape, the fires are inhaled. When the spell is consumed entirely, the Blue Scribes gather the flying daemons into a vast shimmering sphere, distilling the magic they devoured and recording its secrets in their tomes.

THE GOD-HAMMER HIDDEN

The sorcerer Ephryx wagers everything he has to take the ancient city of Elixia, for he has discovered that there lies Ghal Maraz. Unable to claim its magic for himself, he has a grand fortress raised around it and begins to pollute the Hanging Valleys of Anvrok with Tzeentchian magic.

THE INVINCIBLE FORT

Upon the windswept Beastbane Tundra, the Ironjaw tribes erect the Bossfort, an iron castle inviolable even to Ghurish megafauna. Many thousands of orruks gather there, for the fort, built from the remains of the three cities toppled by Gharag Gutslasher, has become famous in greenskin society. Yet word of its construction also reaches Tzeentch. The Pyrofane Cult, newly formed in the cities of the Age of Myth and eager to prove itself, makes its way towards the fort. Having struck a deal with the Grand Cabal, the cult goes in the guise of a roving caravan of Gnoblars. As it passes through the fortress gates, disguises are thrown off and the alliance's glamours discarded to reveal a carnival of colours. Warpfire cascades from the hands of the cultists, consuming the Bossfort's inner walls as the Magisters behind them summon the daemons of the Eternal Conflagration. Before the day is out, the fortress is ablaze with rippling flame that turns flesh and metal alike to tentacled jelly.

The orruks within, crazed with battle-lust, sally forth en masse, hacking hundreds of Kairic Acolytes to pieces before breaking through the ring of blades and flame. The Tzeentch worshippers who survive their onslaught simply walk into the city through the raging inferno, for the flames do not touch them. Over the course of the next week, the Ironjawz find themselves fighting to reclaim their own stronghold while also contending with a moat of fire and mutant flesh. As the flames rage ever higher, the Bossfort is reduced to a bubbling, molten hellscape. All that is left of the complex is a morass of metal that mars the tundra to this day, still as red-hot as the day it first burned.

THE AGE OF SIGMAR

EPHRYX IN EXILE

As Sigmar's Tempest breaks, the hammer Ghal Maraz is located in Anvrok. Vandus Hammerhand and Thostos Bladestorm lead the assault, and though Ephryx translocates the entire Eldritch Fortress to the upper planes of the Hanging Valleys, his ritual to harness Ghal Maraz is ultimately defeated. The sorcerer, on the brink of earning Tzeentch's eternal favour through having denied Sigmar his legendary hammer for so long, is banished into exile in the Realm of Chaos for losing so potent a relic.

UNSTABLE FOUNDATIONS

Many of Sigmar's free cities are built using realmstone in order to speed their construction. Their foundations are laid down in arcane patterns at the behest of the false architect Valius Maliti – in truth, the daemonic Changeling.

A DREAD SUMMONING

In the fledgling city of Colostrum, a trio of Arcanite mages stows away in a prison cart bound for the Erosian Gaol. Thrown into dank cells, they etch strange sigils on the steelwood walls of their confines, each part of a summoning rite of great potency. At the rite's conclusion, daemon Heralds crawl from the mildewed walls to burn the gaolers to death and melt the bars of the Arcanites' cells, allowing the summoners to inscribe even more arcane diagrams under the cover of the resultant jailbreak. By the time their dark work is uncovered, the entire complex is filled with daemons. Lord-Castellant Herqa leads a counterstrike to contain the infestation, but whenever one Horror is struck down, two more take its place. Anarchy boils in the streets as criminals, then cultists, then daemons rampage high and low.

A GRAND MISDIRECTION

The omens and portents of the Time of Tribulations alert Nagash's enemies to the fact that something vast is nearing fruition in Shyish. Many of the forces sent to tear down Nagashizzar find themselves waylaid or turning upon one another, amongst them the hosts of Lord-Ordinator Vorrus Starstrike and the warqueen Marakarr Blood-Sky. None realise that the entity pulling their strings is the Changeling – for in the necroquake, as in all things, Tzeentch sees great opportunity. A long-standing debt from the Great Horned Rat is called in, and the skaven infiltrate Nagash's great work at the last, corrupting his ritual just as it reaches completion.

THE ARCANUM OPTIMAR

The cataclysm of the necroquake causes a tremendous magical backlash, and many of the most powerful spells cast during this time take on a life of their own. The realms are roamed not only by the living dead but by predatory magical emanations, each of which empowers the Change God in its own way. Tzeentch looks upon his great corruption of Nagash's works, and his laughter echoes across the void.

AETHER WAR

The skies of Chamon are riven by war as the Kharadron Overlords and the Disciples of Tzeentch seek to capitalise on the new status quo.

THE PERIMETER INIMICAL

Tzeentch sends his daemon legions to claim vast swathes of each realm's Perimeter Inimical, where the magic rages strong and the defences of the mortal races are weak. Yet the Lords of Change to whom he has entrusted the duty of their conquest are far from unopposed. Not only do they clash with Slaaneshi forces that would claim these extreme environments for their own, they are also confronted by the Null Myriad, a near-endless legion of Bonereapers to whom magic is but the merest hindrance – and who have a cold vengeance driving them to war.

LORDS OF CHANGE

The Feathered Lords, the Winged Watchers, Lords of Change stride to war surrounded by a prismatic aura of ever-changing magic. These master manipulators wield their arcane powers to advance the myriad plots of Tzeentch; where their gaze falls, it pierces the mind, laying bare the hopes and dreams of all mortals before them.

Crackling with magical energies, a Lord of Change hurls pyrotechnic bolts of wyrdfire or splits reality with a gesture, sending enemies tumbling into the Realm of Chaos. As might be expected from greater daemons of Tzeentch, Lords of Change are mighty spellcasters. Pure eldritch power courses through their bodies as blood pumps through the veins of a mortal. More cunning and aloof than the greater daemons of the other Chaos Gods, Lords of Change revel in looking down on their hapless foes. They use their great feathered pinions to carry them across the battlefield, ensuring that they fight the enemy on their terms – and theirs alone.

Although a Lord of Change typically uses magic and trickery to further its ends, it is still a formidable fighter at need, with talons that can shred shields or pierce even sigmarite armour. Countless heroes have underestimated these strange avian daemons, only to see their lances or swords shatter against their would-be quarry's immortal hide. Yet of all of a Lord of Change's many terrible qualities, the most dangerous are its multilayered cunning and fathomless wisdom. Behind its inscrutable gaze lies a curious and callous mind, deeply intelligent yet as uncaring of consequence as it is fascinated by it. The greater daemon's meddling in mortal affairs is not unlike a child playing upon some gigantic anthill, poking at its inhabitants with a stick and laughing at the hopeless efforts of their defence. Nothing pleases these ancient beings more than to see a world broken then made anew, to redirect the course of a life or history itself, spilling hope upon the ground while raising the ambitions of others to perilous heights.

As the purest manifestations of the Great Conspirator, the Lords of Change are unpredictable and shrewd. Perhaps their greatest weakness is that they are manipulative to the point of compulsiveness, continuing to twist plots long after their objectives have been fulfilled. Many a time has a plan nursed for centuries been completed, only for the end goal to be foiled because the Lord of Change pulling the strings could not cease plucking at the skeins of fate.

The Lords of Change serve as the commanders of Tzeentch's armies. They are erudite tacticians, well versed in countless ploys and stratagems. Untold human champions, armies of the Slaves to Darkness and Arcanite Cults live and die at the whim of Lords of Change, though they may not realise it. When they lead their followers in person, they are lethal indeed.

There are nine different ranks of Lords of Change, all with grandiose titles. While the ranks themselves fluctuate in hierarchical standing, the prefix of Exalted is added to the title of the greater daemon that holds Tzeentch's highest regard at any one time. As the Change God is fickle, however, even the most lauded daemons can fall out of favour in the blink of an eye. It goes without saying that Tzeentch's ranking criteria are indecipherable, often appearing completely arbitrary to even the most sagacious of his minions.

KAIROS FATEWEAVER

Even Tzeentch dares not enter the Well of Eternity, the vast receptacle of knowledge at the heart of the Impossible Fortress. It is the one puzzle that the Great Sorcerer has not been able to solve. In the name of understanding, Tzeentch hurled the Lord of Change known as Kairos into the endless pit. As with all daemons, the Fateweaver was part of his patron god, and Tzeentch hoped that Kairos would learn the Well's secrets on his behalf.

After what seemed an infinite span lost in the depths, Kairos eventually clawed his way back out. He emerged greatly changed, his bifurcated soul epitomised by two distinctly different heads. Now Kairos can perceive things that even Tzeentch cannot. Kairos' right head sees possible futures as clear as day, while his left head sees the past without the petty colourations of perspective or bias. Yet this gift was not without toll, for both of Kairos' heads are now blind to the present.

Kairos cannot see time as it passes, only events that are yet to happen or that have already been. For many ages of mortals, Kairos Fateweaver has sat at Tzeentch's right hand, stirring the Well of Eternity with his mind, whispering secrets of what will be or truths about what has already come to pass. Sometimes Tzeentch tires of unravelling these insights, for Kairos has become overfond of the sound of his own croaking voice. At such times, he sends Kairos into the Mortal Realms to lead an army, recover an artefact or follow some thread of fate through to its end. Although the Oracle of Tzeentch is vulnerable to physical attack – the future does not reveal itself swiftly enough to predict the to and fro of battle – Kairos has an unparalleled knowledge of magic. Tracing burning sigils in the air, the Fateweaver grants foes the gift of mutation or hurls pyrotechnic blasts of warpfire, one head always watching for the moment to twist the fates in his favour as the other learns from the successes and failures of the past.

Lieutenants of the daemonic convocations, the Heralds of Tzeentch help lead the multicoloured hosts to battle. Ambitious and daring, Heralds seek to enact swift and traumatic change, hurling the fires of Tzeentch at their foes before leading the charge, gibbering madly all the way.

Tzeentch created Heralds to lead his foot soldiers. These creatures are more powerful than Horrors and are blessed with independent minds so that they might direct the capering masses. Unlike Horrors, Heralds do not morph into multiple beings when struck down. Instead, the magic of their creation has made them far stronger and more resilient than their smaller kin. Gifted sorcerers, Heralds can summon forth the fires of Tzeentch – wyrdfire of pink or blue – to blast enemies into bubbling pools of living sludge. Many Heralds also carry arcane tomes or scrolls from which they periodically recite incantations, augmenting their sorcerous might. The mere presence of a Herald of Tzeentch increases the abilities of their fellow daemons, mutating them into new and stronger forms and empowering their magic.

FLUXMASTERS

The title of Fluxmaster is borne by those Heralds who ride a Disc of Tzeentch. As they fly across the battlefields at great speed, reality reshapes itself in their wake – they are harbingers of both inevitable change and raw primordial anarchy, devolving matter into boiling ectoplasm. Fluxmasters are often used as messengers and outriders within the armies of Tzeentch. Some lead packs of Screamers in aerial charges on the enemy's flanks or even take them to battle in the skies, attacking the drakes and griffons of the Cities of Sigmar or the Kharadron sky-fleets with equal glee. Others take leadership of groups of their fellow Horrors, using their advantageous position to better augment and direct their charges or confound their foes. Wherever they go, the Fluxmasters leave shimmering trails of disruption that scar reality for years to come.

FATESKIMMERS

Fateskimmers are those Tzeentch Heralds that acquire a Burning Chariot – these conveyances are usually the province of Exalted Flamers, but Tzeentchian daemons are not above stealing from one another. Fateskimmers swoop and dive across the battlefield, borne upon a Disc of Tzeentch that is pulled through the skies by a pair of captive Screamers. These Heralds cackle madly as they unleash fearsome sorceries selected from the most eldritch tomes in their collection. Some, wishing to show that they are no slouches in the arts of war , will smash their contraptions into the enemy lines; the more cautious and controlling Fateskimmers instead lurk upon the battle's edge, yelling orders amidst the madness and change-fire. It is not unknown for Fateskimmers to lead entire formations of Burning Chariots, a force that is almost impossible to stop.

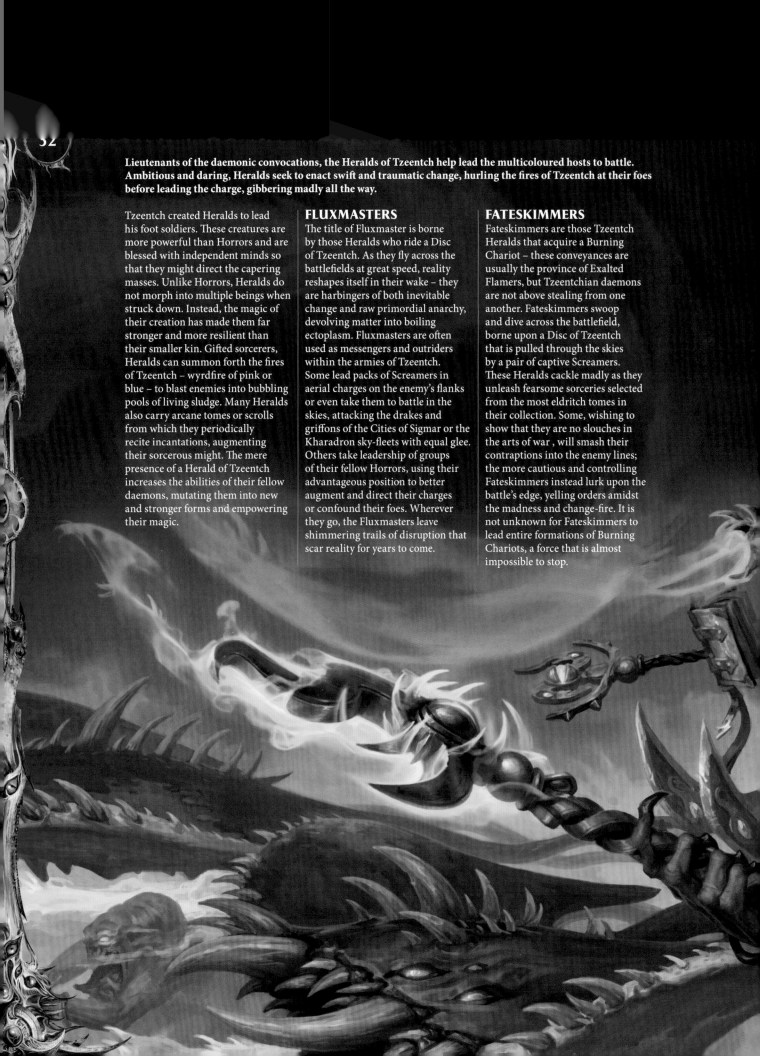

CHANGECASTERS

The most common type of Herald is the Changecaster, named for the mutating magics they wield. Some Changecasters serve in rather menial or frustrating roles in comparison to their mounted equivalents, guarding sources of magical power that Tzeentch deems important to his plans or overseeing repairs within the Crystal Labyrinth. More frequently, these Heralds can be found leading packs of Horrors in a Tzeentchian host, a task much akin to herding an army of maniacal court jesters, for the Horrors are wont to caper off or burst into some questionable display of mischief at any moment. Changecasters have enough of Tzeentch's favour about them to be able to release devastating barrages of magical pyrotechnics, and they are capable fighters despite their gangling, peculiar appearance – they can turn even master swordsmen into mutating slime with a tap of their twisted staves.

DISCS OF TZEENTCH

Each Disc of Tzeentch was once a daemon entity known as a Screamer. The animalistic instincts and fierce predatory nature of these sky-sharks makes them unruly servants, but with the correct transmogrifications, they can be bound to the will of a more powerful being. Their essence hardened and formalised into a shape more pleasing to their master, they become steel-hard discs of daemonic matter that can bear a rider through the air at a dizzying pace. Some are held aloft upon an invisible current of magic, others on tendrils of ectoplasm or writhing forces of antipathy to the realms themselves. Each Disc will have several appendages and protrusions, whether prehensile pseudopods, staring eyestalks or shimmering blades sharp enough to slash open an enemy's throat as the creatures speed past. Only the most talented and determined of Tzeentch's magic users can maintain such a creature's allegiance. Though usually only ridden by daemonic Heralds, there are mortals favoured enough to be borne by these bizarre steeds into war. Those who tame them are given great speed and manoeuvrability. On the peak of Mount Kronus, the Gaunt Summoner known as the Watcher King rode his Disc with such swiftness and surety that he evaded the wrath of Archaon himself – for a time, at least…

FAVOURED SCIONS OF TZEENTCH

There are some amongst Tzeentch's daemon incarnations that have neither the raw power of the greater daemon nor the multitudinous might of his war Heralds, but they have a great impact on his plans nonetheless. These free agents have their own agendas and travel to the ends of the Mortal Realms in furtherance of their esoteric plans.

THE BLUE SCRIBES

Tzeentch created the Blue Horrors P'tarix and Xirat'p to record every spell in existence. Though they are much like their lesser kin in form and surliness, they are far more self-aware and powerful. The pair travel the realms on a broad-winged Disc of Tzeentch, seeking to transcribe every incantation they come across. Each is ever wary of the other's betrayal, for P'tarix can write magical symbols but cannot read, while Xirat'p can read his twin's writing but cannot comprehend it. Squabbling between the two inevitably ensues. If threatened by enemies, Xirat'p reads at random from their accumulated scrolls while P'tarix stabs with his quill, a magical tool crafted from a Lord of Change's pinfeather.

The Blue Scribes' creation is said to date back to a time, aeons ago, when Tzeentch ruled over all. His brothers in darkness, jealous of his supremacy, shattered the Changer of the Ways into countless shards that were scattered across the cosmos. In this way was sorcery brought unto the worlds of mortals. Only by locating and transcribing those fragments, by amassing every spell and soul-splinter in every reality, can the Great Manipulator recover his position as the pre-eminent god of Chaos. To entrust their recovery to a treacherous Lord of Change would be folly; as a result, this nigh impossible task has been given to the Blue Scribes. One day, they will fulfil it, for they are immortal, and they know nothing else.

THE CHANGELING

One of the greatest of Tzeentch's servants, the creature known as the Changeling personifies its patron's aspect as the meddlesome deceiver. It is the trickster supreme, a perfect chameleon whose streak of malice has seen it weave a tapestry of deception and disaster through the history of man, aelf and duardin. Able to shapeshift into any form, not even its fellow Heralds know the daemon's true identity, for it goes cowled and cloaked when not in disguise. Indeed, the Changeling has worn so many different guises throughout the long ages that even it cannot remember its original form.

The Changeling uses manipulation and deception to achieve that which martial strength alone could not. It assumes whatever face will allow it to further its machinations, seamlessly impersonating any other being it chooses, no matter how big or small, mighty or meek. The Changeling has taken the forms of warriors and wizards, master thieves and trusted advisors. Its most recent coup was to impersonate Valius Maliti – the mastermind architect who helped build the foundations of all the Cities of Sigmar. During its time in disguise, the Changeling spread lies and misinformation. It wove webs of falsehood, built many of Sigmar's cities on foundations of disaster and sought out others who might be ambitious enough to be corruptible, planting seeds for future plots.

Sowing discord is what the Changeling does best, and its actions invariably lead to duels, battles and even prolonged wars. Although more an instigator than a fighter, once it abandons its false identity, the Changeling has no qualms about joining the fray personally. It can cast spells to blast the enemy with eldritch fire, and in combat its Trickster Staff adopts the qualities of its opponent's most powerful weapon.

BESTIAL AGENTS OF CHANGE

In Tzeentch's legions, the strange daemons known as Flamers serve as living artillery, blasting foes with gouts of flame before bounding forwards to finish them off. Screamers attack with sharp horns and razored wings, gliding through the air as a sea creature moves through water to swiftly strike anywhere on the foe's battle line.

FLAMERS

Flamers are bizarre creatures, even by the insane standards of the Realm of Chaos. Their tubular bodies randomly sprout gnashing maws and grimacing faces that mimic the last anguished cries of those they have slain. Flamers have no feet; instead, they have an inverted skirt of fungoid flesh that draws in air before expelling it through powerful contractions. Thus, with loud whooshes of discoloured aether, the Flamer can propel itself in leaps and bounds – ungainly perhaps, but capable of a fair turn of speed. Flamers can clear obstacles with ease, and their strange mode of locomotion can even see them bounce across the surface of a body of water, their impacts sending up geysers of steam with each landing.

Although barely sentient, Flamers are extremely dangerous, for they revel in destruction. Some are more capable of independent thought; known as Exalted Flamers, these are champions of their kind and exude sorcery from every pore of their fungoid flesh. They often lead other Flamers or Horrors into battle.

It is the flailing limbs of the Flamer that give the daemon its name. The long appendages end in tooth-lined stumps from which fire spouts. However, these are no normal flames; they are the stuff of raw magic, multicoloured blasts that scorch the senses even as they char the body. Disturbing shapes and apparitions dance in those flames, and they have an unnatural habit of bursting back to life long after they have been stamped out. As the warpfires crackle and hiss, smaller flames spill to the ground and imitate the forms of those nearby. With glee and raucous laughter, these eldritch simulacra mimic their enemies' death throes in a manner that is both mocking and disturbing. Soon, however, the diminutive images fade to nothingness.

SCREAMERS

Screamers are glimmering sky-sharks that ride upon currents of magic as a bird soars upon the breeze. In the Realm of Chaos, they hunt lost souls, but in the Mortal Realms, Screamers gather in undulating shoals and sweep across battlefields, targeting any who have displeased their master, Tzeentch. Festooned with fangs, horns and spurs, they slash foes as they swoop past. When they find a suitable target, the Screamers dive, seeking to tear apart prey with their strange sucking maws lined with razor-sharp teeth. Even large monsters must be particularly wary of shoals of Screamers, for they are capable of gouging out huge chunks of flesh with their lamprey-like mouths.

EXALTED FLAMERS AND BURNING CHARIOTS

The conveyances known as Burning Chariots hurtle through the sky like strangely hued comets. Fiery discs of sorcerous metal shackled to a pair of Screamers, each Burning Chariot is typically commanded by an Exalted Flamer. In times of battle, these chariots trail a wake of warpflame that can immolate those over whom they fly. Those who survive are still not safe, for Burning Chariots enable their riders to bring the gift of change to their enemies with joyous impunity.

HORRORS OF TZEENTCH

Capering, cackling daemons with a cruel sense of humour, the Horrors of Tzeentch embody the maddening inconstancy of the Change God. Even death does not quiet these flame-spewing monsters, as their bodies simply split apart to create smaller, but no less dangerous, fiends.

The Whirling Destroyers, the Bouncing Squealers, the Spinning Sourguts, the Cackling Flames – these are the Horrors of Tzeentch. Horrors are manifestations of pure Chaos, an unbound force that surges forwards, sometimes taking on a discernible form, other times blurring into a frantic mass of glowing colour as they scramble across the battlefield. Luminescent skin and high-pitched squeals of laughter are the hallmarks of Pink Horrors. They twirl and cartwheel frantically, flashes of energy darting from their waving fingertips. In sufficient numbers, these Horrors generate enough magical energy to summon forth the wyrdfires of Tzeentch, which they hurl amidst much giggling to engulf the foe in sheets of magenta flame.

When wounded to death, a Pink Horror exhales a last lunatic cackle before performing a final dramatic act of mayhem. Before the horrified eyes of its foes, the swiftly dissipating ectoplasmic blob of the dying Pink Horror divides, becoming a pair of Blue Horrors. Where there was one, now there are two.

Blue Horrors differ in temperament to their forebears. They are sullen and malicious, wearing perpetual scowls as they sneer and grumble their way through battle. Once spawned, the Blue Horrors fight alongside their fellows, adding a deeper note of morose baritone to the incessant chortling glee of their pink brethren.

As do their larger cousins, when the enemy gets close, the Blue Horrors attempt to strangle their foes with their great, grasping hands. These daemons can likewise conjure flames, though their conflagrations are blue in colour. These too are fires of change and mutation rather than conventional flames; they are as likely to freeze as to burn, to turn back time as to turn flesh to inert crystal or burnished chrome.

To witness such warpfire running wild amongst the ranks is to see a hideous variety of deaths, a horrific tableau of mutations that can steal the sanity of those who behold it. There are times, however, when the flames will heal rather than hurt, for Tzeentch is a fickle god and his plans are often self-defeating. The Horrors themselves are quite used to this; they will reward such instances with sarcastic applause or jeering derision before jetting forth another sheet of warpflame to finish the job.

Should a Blue Horror be cut down, it will emit a drawn-out, fatalistic groan before vanishing in a cloud of daemonic smoke. From those unnatural fumes burst living flames – bright-yellow Brimstone Horrors. Just as two Blue Horrors emerge from each slain Pink Horror, a pair of Brimstone Horrors will emerge from each Blue Horror laid low by a killing strike – and these creatures immediately set about getting revenge on the one responsible for the death of their former incarnation.

These diminutive daemons have a spiteful and vindictive disposition, for, effectively, they have already been killed twice over. They eagerly claw and nip at the enemy with their tiny talons and fangs, hurling sulphurous fire at those who attempt to extricate their ally from the death he so richly deserves. At close quarters, they climb up the legs of their enemies, cackling in mean-spirited glee while making every attempt to set their adversaries alight before they themselves finally gutter and burn out.

MORTAL MASTERS OF THE ARCANE

The leaders of the Arcanite Cults are more than mere dabblers in the eldritch arts; they are amongst the most gifted spellcasters in all the Mortal Realms. These are souls both blessed and cursed; their burning need to know the secrets of reality and to profit from their talents has given them power – but at the cost of much of their sanity.

MAGISTERS

The nefarious spiders at the centre of an Arcanite Cult's web, Magisters are among the most powerful of Tzeentch's mortal servants. Each is a warlock of rare and terrible potency. With an arcane gesture, a Magister summons roaring flames of every colour or sends out rays of pure change-magic that mutate their enemies into whimpering lumps of flesh. To annoy a Magister is to court a strange and excruciating demise.

A reservoir of the raw essence of Chaos crackles within each Magister. The Architect of Fate is eager to bless his servants with all manner of mutations: third eyes, avian features, extra limbs and stranger gifts besides are all common 'rewards'. Alongside these physical aberrations, Magisters wield a warpsteel sword and Tzeentchian runestaff. Through these they direct the unbound potential of change itself; those who drink from this font of power too eagerly find themselves reduced to hideous Spawn. Still, Tzeentch demands unlimited ambition from his Magisters, and the lure of daemonhood is a prize they will go to any length to claim.

Though Tzeentch favours labyrinthine cunning over martial strength, on many occasions a Magister will judge it necessary to contribute their own magical might to battle. The largest Arcanite Cults may contain multiple Magisters; often each of these sorcerers will possess their own grandiose title, such as Grand Vizier of Change or Exalted Potentate of Transformation, and all constantly endeavour to undermine or manipulate their rivals. Only through such guile can they advance to the upper echelons of the cabal's hierarchy. Tzeentch, of course, looks upon this treachery with approval, so long as it does not interfere with his mercurial schemes.

MAGISTERS ON DISCS OF TZEENTCH

Magisters who establish their power base in the most Chaos-tainted regions of the realms – or those who simply revel in the unsubtle destruction of their foes – bind Screamers into their service as Discs of Tzeentch. This is no easy task, and overconfident Magisters often find themselves shredded by the primal daemon they sought to control, whether through an error in their own ritual preparations or through the machinations of a resourceful underling.

Those who succeed are rewarded with a swift mode of transport and deadly edge in battle alike. From atop the creature's circular body, the Magister can unleash ruinous spells of destruction, while enemies that stray too close are cut to ribbons by the Disc's razor-sharp teeth and horns as it spins mindlessly at its master's command.

FATEMASTERS

A Fatemaster is a Chaos Lord dedicated to Tzeentch, as much a ferocious armoured bladesman as a gifted manipulator of destiny. Some Fatemasters command entire Arcanite Cults, others lead covens, while some perform more specialised roles, such as enforcer, Keeper of the Realmgate or doomsayer.

To attain the rank of Fatemaster, a warrior must not only prove their devotion to Tzeentch, they must also show the cunning and quick thinking favoured by the Changer of the Ways. After all, the Arcanite Cults are Tzeentch's chosen; these are not foul-smelling and barbaric Slaves to Darkness armies but erudite and clandestine warriors fighting a guerrilla war, often ensconced deep within enemy-held territory. Indeed, an aspiring Fatemaster must undertake trials that would certainly kill lesser men.

More than mere bravery and martial skill are required to pass the dreaded Nine Trials of Fate. It takes either an incredible amount of luck or intuition that surpasses anticipation. To duck the sweeping blade that moves faster than human reaction, to espy the treacherous ally before their betrayal – these are necessary not just to succeed in the trials but also to survive them. Those few who complete the tasks are anointed Fatemasters and sent to lead the secret enclaves of the Arcanite Cults. Before they do so, however, they are gifted mighty boons: a fireglaive, a soulbound shield, Chaos armour and a Disc of Tzeentch.

In battle, a Fatemaster streaks into the fray, leaving behind a wake of dismembered corpses – the gruesome aftermath of precision glaive-strikes and swooping dives from the bladed Disc they ride. Hostile spells drizzle like water from a Fatemaster's gleaming shield. Perhaps their most powerful gift is the fate-shifting aura – the ability to twist the very laws of causality in Tzeentch's favour, causing enemy arrows to hit armour rather than flesh, empowering an ally's spells or guiding friendly blades to strike home instead of glancing astray.

CURSELINGS

Instantly recognisable by the cackling homunculus that sprouts from their torsos, Curselings are favoured lieutenants in many Arcanite Cults. Guided by the misshapen beings melded to them, Curselings use their many dark blessings to further a ceaseless quest for arcane knowledge.

Few of Tzeentch's gifts can be understood, for the Dark God's true will is beyond the ken of mortalkind. So it is with Curselings, those beings sometimes known as the Eyes of Tzeentch. Once, they were rising sorcerers, acolytes of the dark arts who sought to further their arcane studies, but the cost of their curiosity soon became clear. The secrets they had garnered coalesced inside their bodies, forming eldritch tumours of forbidden knowledge that grew and grew. Each was possessed by a malign sentience: a spirit creature from the Realm of Chaos known as a Tretchlet. Like a monstrous parasite, this fiend grows from the body of its host and gives constant hissing advice to gather further knowledge. The Tretchlet's Curse is thought to afflict those who learn one secret too many – or perhaps just the wrong one at the wrong time.

Regardless, Curselings are highly coveted by Arcanite Cults. Acting as lieutenants for their cabals, Curselings sometimes fulfil the role of inquisitor, for their physical form is mighty and Tretchlets can detect lies. Sucking air through their teeth, the grotesque beings can taste secrets and their questions draw out hidden knowledge – invaluable traits to cults seeking arcane enlightenment. A trial by Curseling is also an effective way of determining whether new acolytes are worthy of joining a cult.

Though they excel in the role of lie-seeker, all Curselings hunger for battle. They prove formidable warriors on the battlefield, but they are most valued for the Tretchlet's ability to glean an enemy wizard's spells and hurl them back at the caster. Nothing gives a Tretchlet more gratification – or makes it cackle more maniacally – than when it slays a wizard with their own spells.

KAIRIC ACOLYTES

Kairic Acolytes are the human cultists of Tzeentch, they who speak the killing words, the Chanters of Change, the Altered. They are cunning infiltrators who have made dire sacrifices in exchange for knowledge and power, and they walk amongst the unsuspecting folk until the time for them to strike is ripe.

These robed cultists chant not in a tribal rhythm that stirs the blood but in a dark tongue that chills it. From disturbing to painful, the tone fluctuates; the cadence halts, begins and grates. From this dissonance, each Acolyte summons a radiant ball of scintillating light. For an instant, the spheres hang in mid-air, then they streak off towards their target in a roaring volley of sorcerous bolts. Those who become Kairic Acolytes come from all walks of life, whether tribesmen led astray by an arcane calling, seekers of forbidden knowledge or city-dwelling civil servants overeager to gain power. All share a driving ambition that sets them apart from the common man. It is not by chance that such individuals cross paths with undercover Acolytes, for the Arcanite Cults target and recruit aspirants with great care, taking years or even decades to ensnare potential supplicants. Given time, those who listen to their night-time whisperings will one day serve the Architect of Fate.

In the end, only those who wholly commit can attempt the Kairic Test of Nine. Each cult has its own variations on these rites, but all end with the walk through warpfire. Those that emerge unharmed become Kairic Acolytes. Chanting arcane phrases that hurt the ears of the uninitiated, a scrawny scribe or frail council elder transforms. Flesh ripples and from nothing appear a curseblade and shearbeak helm, gleaming greaves and an Arcanite shield. Thus can a cultist, with mere words, transform themselves from ailing scholar or lanky apprentice to a muscular ideal of the human form and back again. With such arcane disguises, the Kairic Acolytes can infiltrate and subvert the very forces of those who hunt them.

LORDS OF THE SILVER TOWERS

Ogroid Thaumaturges are hulking, fearsome mages with runes carved into their muscle-bound frames. Their masters are the legendary Gaunt Summoners of the Silver Towers. Unlike their minions, these daemon spellcasters prefer to fight from afar, their spells able to twist landscapes and immolate armies with wyrdfire.

OGROID THAUMATURGES

Shrouded in mystery and rumour, little is actually known about Ogroid Thaumaturges, though there is much speculation. There is no doubt, however, that the creatures are steeped in magic – their very skin writhes with arcane energies as inner fires blaze eldritch sigils across their hulking bodies.

These creatures like to think of themselves as cerebral and sophisticated, but when they are wounded or confounded, they reveal something of the terrifying beast within. In their rage, the telltale multicoloured flames of Tzeentch erupt about them, often centred around their totemic staves. For all their protestations to the contrary, for all their pretensions and use of sophisticated language, Ogroid Thaumaturges are essentially bestial in nature, possessed of enough strength to tear a man in two with their bare hands or drive their horns through even sigmarite plate armour.

Although their might rivals that of a troggoth, Ogroid Thaumaturges are indeed sorcerous beings possessed of cunning minds. It is said that they know more of the secrets of wyrdflame than any save the most accomplished spellcasters. They can summon coruscating blasts of the mutating fire from which Tzeentch's own daemons spring forth, a sure sign of the Change God's favour – for, in truth, these strange horned monsters are truer reflections of Tzeentch's form than any Kairic mage. Ogroid Thaumaturges are especially revered in the Pyrofane Cult, where their flame powers are greatly venerated by the Kairic Acolytes. Some Ogroid Thaumaturges lead a coven to battle, with Tzaangors in particular flocking to the horned giants, while others serve as bodyguards for the enigmatic Gaunt Summoners.

GAUNT SUMMONERS

Of the ranks of Tzeentchian sorcerers, there are few higher than the dreaded Gaunt Summoners. Each of their number is a daemon monarch, a creature of fable and myth that can single-handedly shift the tide of a battle. Luckily for Sigmar and his allies, however, there are but nine such beings in existence, elevated to their lofty station by the Architect of Fate himself. Upon achieving that terrifying level of accomplishment, each Gaunt Summoner was gifted with even greater arcane power, a changestaff, a flying Disc of Tzeentch and the key to one of the nine Silver Towers.

The Silver Towers are insanely complex labyrinths, realities folded into one another each replete with puzzle-fortresses beyond the scope of mortal minds. As a pastime, the Gaunt Summoners delight in snatching up those travellers foolish enough to risk journeying through Chaos-corrupted Realmgates. Such captives awaken in the labyrinthine corridors, impossible dimensions and ever-shifting pathways of the Silver Towers. The Gaunt Summoner watches with amusement as its puppets are slain in an infinite number of ways by lethal creatures and devious traps. Those few who fight their way to freedom are granted boons, but such an occurrence is rare indeed.

When taking to the battlefield alongside an Arcanite Cult, the Gaunt Summoners are regarded with a level of awe normally reserved for Lords of Change. With but a word, these master sorcerers can call forth daemons from nearby Realmgates and weak spots in reality or cripple the enemy by turning their own mental strength against them.

Once, the Gaunt Summoners were given freedom by Tzeentch to pursue their own fates. In this, the god was wise, as each of the mage-lords was obsessed with the accumulation of magical knowledge and power. Through these pursuits, they brought Tzeentch great glory. Even the Gaunt Summoners' amusements – testing the mettle of warriors in their endless labyrinths – offered the Changer of the Ways occasional distraction. Yet Archaon, most powerful champion of Chaos, wished to possess the eldritch power of the Gaunt Summoners for his own.

Tzeentch watched with great interest as Archaon sacrificed the lives of many of his followers seeking to discover the true names of the Gaunt Summoners, the only way in which to bind them to his service. Tzeentch was of two minds as to who to aid in this power struggle. The Gaunt Summoners belonged to him, yet, on the other hand, the attempts of each of the Dark Gods to persuade the Everchosen to serve them exclusively, rather than all of them equally, had failed thus far. This both vexed and impressed Tzeentch, for it was not often that another could dictate the Great Conspirator's chosen course of action. In the end, Tzeentch reasoned that allowing Archaon to usurp dominion of the nine daemon-sorcerers would better serve the god's own ends. So Archaon went on to win the names of all the Gaunt Summoners, never realising the subtle aid from which he benefited along the way. Ever since, the Gaunt Summoners have chafed beneath the rule of Archaon, and they plot to one day rebel and claim his throne. After all, change is inevitable…

TZAANGORS

Tzaangors are savage, avian beast-kin dedicated to Tzeentch. As such, they have been warped into shapes more pleasing to the Architect of Fate. Foes that underestimate the bestial cunning and fierce strength of the Tzaangors quickly fall before their sharp blades, piercing beaks and gouging horns.

Strange trilling calls come from seemingly deserted woodlands and flying shapes flit through sudden mists. Peering out from illusion-concealed lairs, the Tzaangors watch and wait. Although rarely seen, they have been massing their numbers throughout the ages, establishing strongholds and launching covert strikes to further the aims of their patron god. Soon, the time will be ripe for conquest, and they will rise to unleash their full fury.

Tzaangor origins are as multifarious as the plans of Tzeentch themselves. Some are gor-kin who have been corrupted – or elevated, they might say – by a Tzaangor Shaman; others are humans who have undergone horrific rituals. Others still are beast-children, mutants born of human parents and left to die, but instead found and raised by Arcanite Cults. Regardless of source, all recognise that they have been blessed by Tzeentch. Tzaangors are far more intelligent than other beastmen and look down upon their beast-kin, seeing themselves as evolved and their cousins as little more than brute animals. The strangely mutated minds of Tzaangors have become particularly attuned to magic and they are drawn to the arcane, seeking to hoard it. Tzaangors are also closely bound to the strands of fate, their animal instincts able to detect omens the way beasts scent prey upon the winds. Yet Tzeentch did not transform his chosen beastmen to seek magic alone – he also created them to kill.

Many rituals prepare Tzaangors for war, culminating in the weapon-taking rite where the rent armour and broken weapons of foes are transformed into the resplendent gear worthy of fighters of Tzeentch. In battle, the Tzaangor warflocks are led by a Twistbray champion; they fight with savage skill, stabbing and hacking with curved swords or axes as well as rending with horn and beak. As magical creatures, they draw energy from the proximity of Tzeentchian sorcery and others of their kind. Favoured Tzaangors are sometimes honoured with bearing their god's icon to war. These ornate totems can absorb the magical energies of nearby spellcasters and are used by the Tzaangors to steal the arcane force that they use to grow their magical Herdstones, known as flux-cairns. Recently tapped eldritch powers can even be directed as bolts towards nearby foes. Those Tzaangors whose deeds have caught the eye of their patron are rewarded with divine blessings. They are divided into two distinct groups, the Enlightened and the Skyfires.

TZAANGOR ENLIGHTENED

The proud yet twisted Enlightened carry spears wrought of change-metal. They possess the strange ability to perceive echoes of past events around them, no matter how well those truths might be hidden. In combat, their foes are driven to distraction and despair as their darkest secrets are squawked out by the chattering Enlightened. An enemy with much to hide may find his allies forsaking him at a critical moment – or might simply find himself unmanned by the knowledge that his innermost secrets are known to his foes. The Enlightened take great pleasure in revealing their victims' secrets, whether marching to war amongst their lesser kin to inspire them to greater acts of savagery or riding high on scintillating Discs of Tzeentch. This same visionary power allows them to take advantage of their enemies' past mistakes; picking out their weak spots, reopening old wounds and exploiting gaps in their guard can see a hidden flaw turned into a critical disadvantage. In such a manner do these Tzaangors turn the slightest self-defeating tendencies of their enemies into fatal weaknesses.

TZAANGOR SKYFIRES

Skyfires soar through the burning skies upon their Discs of Tzeentch, letting fly their arrows of fate at those who threaten Tzeentch's plans. It is their gift to see potential futures, but it is their curse that they can never speak of them. In contrast to their garrulous Enlightened brethren, Skyfires are utterly silent, barring the twang of their bowstrings as they loose their twisting shafts. By scrying the possibilities laid before them on the field of battle, they fire each arrow on a seemingly aimless trajectory, only for their target to lunge, be tripped or find himself wrong-footed right into the path of the Tzaangor's shot. The magical arrow penetrates gaps in armour or scaled skin as effectively as the foil of any master swordsman, and the fate the Skyfire has foreseen is made clear.

TZAANGOR SHAMANS

The Shamans of the Tzaangor are the most powerful of their kind, gifted by the Great Conspirator with arcane abilities, precognitive visions and high intelligence. They begrudge all who are not Tzaangors, using their transmogrifying powers to mutate their foes and redress the balance.

Those destined to become Tzaangor Shamans are born amongst dark omens, such as massed mutant births, the rising of strange stars and confluences of magical power. As a mark of their greatness, Tzaangor Shamans are gifted a Disc of Tzeentch, which raises them literally as well as symbolically above their bestial kin. Tzaangor Shamans are revered by their warflocks, for they see the Shaman as holding the greatest of boons – the ability to transmute other beings into Tzaangors. With a defiant hoofstomp and a crack of their staff, the Shaman unleashes their mutagenic spell. Those struck by the blue-tinged bolt fall to the ground, writhing uncontrollably and wracked with agonising contortions. Their skulls split as sharp beaks push forth, worm-like tongues wriggling within. Arms elongate and sprout rough spines, eyes turn red and skin shimmers blue. Before long, the stricken target rises once more as a glistening Tzaangor, ready to join the Shaman's ranks and embrace his new master, Tzeentch, with body and soul.

Transmogrification is not a Shaman's only power; they also possess the gift of prophecy. Other Tzaangors believe that, when in a trance, the Shamans spirit-walk into the Realm of Chaos to take commands from the Feathered Lords themselves.

Upon emerging from such catatonic states, many Tzaangor Shamans find new purpose. They may migrate from their flock, following a divine calling. Some leave to join a different Arcanite Cult, others to lead a coven upon some sacred mission. Those who remain continue to head the warflocks, guiding them through many fell rites while directing the raising of flux-cairns. It was the Shamans who first showed the warflocks the wisdom of eating the tongues of their foes to gain their speech and insight. It is they who lead the hunt for Chaos creatures, subduing such monsters as Cockatrices or Mutalith Vortex Beasts to mark their hides with the Dark Tongue, and it is they who know the secrets of distilling the blood of mages to boost the potency of their own spells.

In battle, Tzaangor Shamans are no frail wizards. These bestial mystics swoop directly into the fray, slashing at the foe with ritual daggers and rending their flesh with wicked beaks and horns in the name of almighty Tzeentch.

THE EYES OF THE NINE

Vortemis the All-Seeing, his Tzaangor lieutenant K'charik and the twin Kairic Acolytes Narvia and Turosh have long roamed the Mirrored City of Shadespire. They serve at the will of the Gaunt Summoners, the nine masters of the mysterious Silver Towers. Ever since the city fell, Vortemis has sought to open a portal between hidden Shadespire and one of those twisted, labyrinthine fortresses. All his efforts have thus far been in vain. Yet with the unravelling of magic that has redefined the Mortal Realms, a new opportunity has arisen. The Eyes of the Nine now seek to convert captured shadeglass relics into beacons of arcane power, sorcerous lodestones that will anchor Shadespire to the Silver Towers and spill forth the madness of the Realm of Chaos. Should they succeed, Tzeentch will surely claim dominion over the Mirrored City entire.

High amongst the floating islands of the Spiral Crux, a war for reality itself rages between the Disciples of Tzeentch and the Kharadron Overlords native to Chamon.

THE ELDRITCH HOSTS

A riot of colour replete with arcane symbols and a dizzying variety of anatomies, the Disciples of Tzeentch are a mesmerising sight as they bring the blessed change of Tzeentch to their foes. Here we present a showcase of Disciples of Tzeentch models expertly painted by Games Workshop's own 'Eavy Metal and Design Studio army painters.

Across the realms, there are countless mortal agents bringing the will of the Changer of the Ways to fruition, each thinking themselves a key part of Tzeentch's plan. All too often they are the tools of a far greater mind – that of a Lord of Change.

Kairos Fateweaver

Magister

Vortemis the All-Seeing

Tzaangor Shaman

Tzaangor Mutant and Tzaangor Icon Bearer

Tzaangor of the Twisted Fate

Tzaangor Twistbray with paired savage blades

After inciting a riot among the ruins of Elixia – and, in doing so, forcing the Celestial Vindicators into a costly purge – the Arcanites reveal themselves as the architects of their foe's misfortune.

Fateskimmer, Herald of Tzeentch on Burning Chariot

The borders of Tzeentch's daemon realm encroach on the lands of mortals, where cunning and duplicitous Heralds of Tzeentch infest the ground itself with the mutating energies of change. To fight back is to be forever cursed.

Surging from an underground crevasse in the Hinterlands of Ghur, an Exalted Flamer leads a spearhead of its kin to cleanse the dank caves of the Underguts Mawtribe with searing, mutagenic flame.

Burning Chariot of Tzeentch

The Deathrattle legions bound to defend Prosperia finally meet their match when a Magister leads his Tzaangor flock against them. Driven by Tzeentch's will, the cold malice of the dead is nothing to the burning fires of change.

Blue Horrors

Brimstone Horrors

Changecaster, Herald of Tzeentch

Iridescent Horror and Pink Horror Icon Bearer

Tzaangor Skyfire

Aviarch

Tzaangor Skyfire

Tzaangor Enlightened on Discs of Tzeentch

The Changeling

Curseling, Eye of Tzeentch

Gaunt Summoner

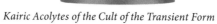

Kairic Acolytes of the Cult of the Transient Form

Kairic Acolyte with cursed blade and Arcanite shield

Kairic Acolyte of the Pyrofane Cult

Kairic Acolyte of the Guild of Summoners

The sky-borne aether-gold of Griffon's Eyrie brings profiteering Kharadron into the lair of Magister Ab-het and his daemons, where magic hangs thick in the air. Few will return, and those who do will be changed inside and out.

The Blue Scribes

Magister on Disc of Tzeentch

The swirling portal of the Banelands, corrupted by Tzeentch's will, has long been concealed by the Changeling's illusions.
Though the Stormcast Eternals move to close it down, daemons already gather thick around it.

Pyrocaster

Flamers of Tzeentch

Exalted Flamer of Tzeentch

Screamer of Tzeentch

Ogroid Thaumaturge

The orruks of the Ironsunz tribe return to their Ghurish encampment, only to find their sacred idol has been profaned by an Ogroid Thaumaturge. A fight to the death is soon to follow, but the Tzeentchian mage has allies close at hand.

MAGIC AND MUTATION

The variety of units, spells and abilities available to a Disciples of Tzeentch player is impressive. With a little forward scheming, you can form a warhost shaped to a particular play style – or just collect the units that catch your eye and, like a true scion of change, adapt from there. We have put together an army by way of an example.

When deciding which units to include in your Disciples of Tzeentch host, you might base your collection on the appearance of the models, how they will perform on the tabletop, or a piece of lore found in a battletome, novel or setting of your own creation. Wherever you take your inspiration from, there is no single right way to collect an army – only the way that you deem best. The goal is always the same: to field a force of Disciples ready to shape reality to your whims. Here are a few insights into how we assembled the collection below.

The siren call of magical dominance leads many players to specialise in the casting of spectacular spells, many and often, and that can be tremendous fun. However, such a singular approach has dangers as well as opportunities. In the first turn, your heroes may not be in range to capitalise upon those deadly skills, and if you find yourself playing an army that is skilled at unbinding, your carefully made plans may come apart. Instead, we've constructed an army that can fight, shoot, cast magic and manoeuvre at speed, allowing us to adapt and

change our plans as the dice fall where they may (or get altered by our Destiny Dice if we really need them to play ball). This means a loss of raw firepower in some situations, but it will enable us to have a good chance of victory in any scenario, especially one where objectives are placed in the middle of the board.

Our first port of call was to choose our sub-faction – in this case, the Cult of the Transient Form. We have a whole flock of Tzaangors on standby for when our Kairic Acolytes die (and they will), in case

they are lucky enough to benefit from the Change-gift ability. After amassing a couple of decent units of Acolytes, we put together a massive unit of Horrors. This will be used to anchor our centre, because when these models die, they can increase their numbers. This means they are great at claiming objectives even in death and they are very difficult to shift. With the battleline units sorted, along with a decent amount of shooting-phase firepower, we wanted to include some serious magical clout. Enter Kairos Fateweaver, perhaps the most impressive model in the range. Backed up by a Changecaster and an Ogroid Thaumaturge, he will ensure we have magical dominance and a bit of punch in close combat if all else fails. Two Burning Chariots and a unit of Flamers of Tzeentch gives us some great mid-range firepower, with three Skyfires picking out juicy targets with their Arrows of Fate. A unit of Screamers will operate nearby, able to dart in to slow down (and possibly slash to death) any fast-moving threats to our spellcasters. Our overall play style will be mobile, keeping at medium range and harassing the enemy's primary threat before moving on to the next once it's out of the picture. Should the enemy push through our firepower, we will throw in the Horrors and Kairic Acolytes to occupy them until we can redeploy. With both units potentially getting even more deadly the more they take damage, our opponent will have their hands full, allowing us to shape the game with spells and pinpoint attacks until victory is secured in the name of Almighty Tzeentch.

1. Kairos Fateweaver
2. Ogroid Thaumaturge
3. Changecaster, Herald of Tzeentch
4. Burning Chariot of Tzeentch
5. Exalted Flamer of Tzeentch
6. Burning Chariot of Tzeentch
7. Flamers of Tzeentch
8. Horrors of Tzeentch
9. Screamers of Tzeentch
10. Tzaangor Skyfires
11. Kairic Acolytes
12. Kairic Acolytes

'You think yourself immune to the change you fear? You think by stubbornly reinforcing the old ways, by clinging to the comfort of the past, you can slow down the evolution of the cosmos? Simpleton! Only by embracing the flux that will consume us all can you hope to survive it. Your former incarnation will die, of course, but you shall live anew...'
- Magister Lucidan Ararzh

PAINTING YOUR DISCIPLES OF TZEENTCH

A Disciples of Tzeentch army is an exciting painting challenge whether you are a veteran hobbyist or you have never picked up a paintbrush in your life. On the following pages, you will find stage-by-stage guides to help you make the most of your Disciples of Tzeentch Citadel Miniatures, with tips and examples from the experts.

There is nothing like the sight of a fully painted army of Citadel Miniatures, and a vibrant host of Tzeentch can be a wonderful thing to behold. There is real satisfaction to be had in adding colour to your collection, teasing out the finely sculpted details, making your miniatures your own and creating a unified force. After all, one painted model looks great, but an entire army brought together through shared colours, iconography and ornate heraldry is even better.

Before painting your models, you'll first need to assemble them. To begin with, we suggest you follow the advice given in the construction booklet provided with your models.

There's no right or wrong way to go about painting your collection of miniatures. Some people revel in treating each miniature as a work of art, lavishing attention on every millimetre of every model and painstakingly crafting scenic bases. Others prefer a far simpler approach with basic but consistent paint jobs that allow them to quickly complete legions of warriors. And, of course, there is plenty of middle ground for those who enjoy painting their troops but want to devote special attention to key figures such as a Lord of Change. Again, there is no one way to paint, just the way that works best for you. In the end, the goal is to field a fully painted Disciples of Tzeentch army on the tabletop.

On the following pages, you will find step-by-step guides, variant colour schemes and top tips to inspire you as you paint your Tzeentchian host.

WARHAMMER TV

Warhammer TV's painting tutorials have insights for everyone as they show you how to paint Citadel Miniatures from start to finish. The guides are available for free on games-workshop.com and can also be watched via the Warhammer TV YouTube channel. Why not take a moment to check them out?

BRIMSTONE HORRORS

Over a Corax White undercoat, apply a basecoat of Yriel Yellow.

Once that is dry, apply an all-over shade of Fuegan Orange.

Carefully apply a chunky highlight of Fire Dragon Bright.

Apply a second highlight of Evil Sunz Scarlet, focused towards the tips of the flames.

Next, apply a fine highlight of Abaddon Black at the very edges of the flames.

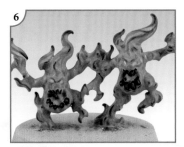
Finally, add some White Scar to the eyes and inside of the mouth, then paint the teeth Abaddon Black.

PINK HORROR SKIN

1 Apply a 1:2 mix of Volupus Pink and Contrast Medium over a Corax White undercoat.

2 Next, apply a layer of Emperor's Children onto the raised areas, leaving the recesses as they are.

3 Apply a chunky highlight of Fulgrim Pink, being careful not to get bitten in the process.

4 Finally, apply a few coats of Carroburg Crimson to the ends of the hands, feet and tentacles.

BLUE HORROR SKIN

1 Apply a 1:4 mix of Talassar Blue and Contrast Medium over a Corax White undercoat.

2 Apply a 1:2 mix of Akhelian Green and Contrast Medium to the hands, feet and ends of the tentacles.

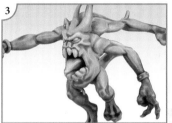

3 Add a fine highlight of Blue Horror to the main body and Lothern Blue to the darker parts.

HORROR DETAILS

Base: Naggaroth Night.
Highlight: Xereus Purple with a dot of Genestealer Purple.

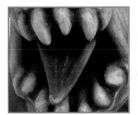

Base: Wraithbone.
Contrast: Skeleton Horde.
Highlight: Screaming Skull.

Base: Averland Sunset.
Shade: Fuegan Orange.
Highlight: Yriel Yellow.

Base: Runefang Steel.
Shade: Biel-Tan Green.
Highlight: Stormhost Silver.

SCREAMERS

Base: Rhinox Hide.
Highlight: Gorthor Brown, Baneblade Brown.

Base: Abaddon Black.
Highlight: Eshin Grey, then Dawnstone.

Use the same process as the Horror eyes above, adding a triangle of Abaddon Black for the pupil.

GAUNT SUMMONER SKIN

1 Over a Chaos Black undercoat, apply a basecoat of The Fang.

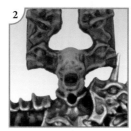

2 Carefully apply a layer of Russ Grey, avoiding the recesses.

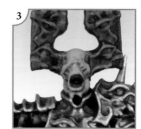

3 Next, apply a chunky highlight of Fenrisian Grey.

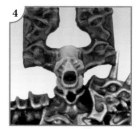

4 Finally, add some fine highlights of Pallid Wych Flesh.

GAUNT SUMMONER CLOTH

1 Apply a basecoat of Kantor Blue.

2 Apply Alaitoc Blue to the lower half of the cloth.

3 Apply Lothern Blue to the very bottom of the cloth.

4 Finally, highlight with Temple Guard Blue.

GAUNT SUMMONER GOLD

1 Over an undercoat of Chaos Black, apply a basecoat of Retributor Armour.

2 Apply an all-over shade of Agrax Earthshade, then leave it to dry thoroughly.

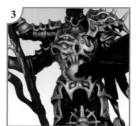

3 Carefully apply a layer of Auric Armour Gold, avoiding the recesses.

4 Edge highlight the raised areas with Runefang Steel.

GAUNT SUMMONER BOOK

1 Basecoat the pages with two thin coats of Rakarth Flesh.

2 Apply a layer of Ushabti Bone, avoiding the recesses.

3 Highlight the edges of the pages with Pallid Wych Flesh.

4 Add some lines of text and chaotic patterns using Rhinox Hide.

TZAANGOR SKIN

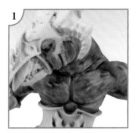

1

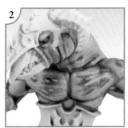

2

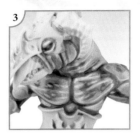

3

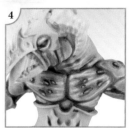

4

Apply a 1:4 mix of Ultramarine Blue and Contrast Medium.

Apply a layer of Fenrisian Grey, leaving the recesses as dark areas.

Next, apply a fine highlight of Ulthuan Grey to define the musculature.

Paint on feathers using Screamer Pink, Ungor Flesh and Squig Orange.

DISC OF TZEENTCH

1

2

3

First, undercoat the Disc with Leadbelcher.

Apply a shade of Druchii Violet to the interior areas.

Add a layer of Retributor Armour to the raised ornamentation.

4

5

6

Apply a shade of Reikland Fleshshade to the gold areas.

Highlight the gold areas with Liberator Gold.

Finally, give the Disc an all-over drybrush of Necron Compound.

TZAANGOR DETAILS

Base: Wraithbone.
Contrast: Skeleton Horde.
Highlight: Screaming Skull.

Base: XV-88.
Shade: Agrax Earthshade.
Highlight: Karak Stone, Screaming Skull.

Base: Squig Orange.
Shade: Carroburg Crimson.
Highlight: Ungor Flesh.

Base: Runefang Steel.
Shade: Druchii Violet.
Highlight: Stormhost Silver.

LORD OF CHANGE SKIN

1 Give the model an undercoat of Macragge Blue.

2 Basecoat the blue skin with Kantor Blue.

3 Apply a shade of Drakenhof Nightshade to the skin.

4 Apply a drybrush of Imrik Blue to the skin.

5 Next, apply a light drybrush of Skink Blue followed by Ulthuan Grey.

6 Finally, apply a 1:5 mix of Talassar Blue and Contrast Medium to the skin.

LORD OF CHANGE WINGS

1 Apply a basecoat of Screamer Pink to the wing feathers.

2 Using an L Dry brush, dab Pink Horror on the lower parts of the feathers. This is known as 'stippling'.

3 Stipple Cadian Fleshtone below the Pink Horror, taking care to make the gradation gradual.

4 Next, stipple Kislev Flesh on the outermost parts of the feathers, again ensuring a gradual transition of colour.

Shade all over with a 1:1 mix of Druchii Violet and Lahmian Medium.

Finally, apply a light drybrush of Eldar Flesh and prepare thyself to receive Tzeentch's blessing.

LORD OF CHANGE PALE SKIN

Apply a basecoat of Celestra Grey to the chest, neck and legs.

Apply a 1:5 mix of Talassar Blue and Contrast Medium.

Apply a layer of Ulthuan Grey, avoiding the recesses.

Finally, apply a fine highlight of White Scar to define the muscles.

LORD OF CHANGE BEAK

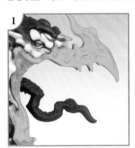

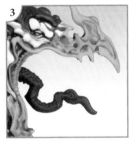

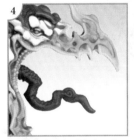

Basecoat with Averland Sunset.

Shade with Reikland Fleshshade.

Highlight with Ungor Flesh.

Apply a fine highlight of Screaming Skull.

LORD OF CHANGE DETAILS

Base: Screamer Pink.
Shade: Nuln Oil.
Highlight: Pink Horror, Emperor's Children.

Base: Rakarth Flesh.
Shade: Agrax Earthshade.
Highlight: Pallid Wych Flesh.

Base: Celestra Grey.
Contrast: 1:4 mix Talassar Blue/Contrast Medium.
Highlight: Ulthuan Grey.

Base: Yriel Yellow.
Shade: Fuegan Orange.
Highlight: Screaming Skull.

ACOLYTE LIGHT SKIN

1

2

3

Apply Guilliman Flesh over a Grey Seer basecoat.

Add a layer of Rakarth Flesh to the raised areas.

Highlight with Pallid Wych Flesh.

Top Tips: It is good practice to apply a coat of Munitorum Varnish spray to protect your models against the wear and tear of battle! You can use a pot of Stormshield instead if you want to target specific areas.

ACOLYTE DARK SKIN

1

2

3

4

Base with Catachan Fleshtone.

Layer with Bloodreaver Flesh.

Highlight with Knight-Questor Flesh.

Apply some fine highlights of Cadian Fleshtone.

ACOLYTE CLOTH

1

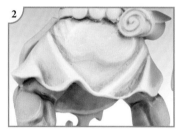
2

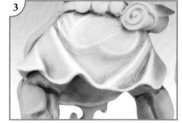
3

Apply a 2:1 mix of Lahmian Medium and Drakenhof Nightshade to the deepest recesses.

Apply a chunky highlight of Ulthuan Grey to the raised areas of cloth.

Add a very fine highlight of White Scar to the raised edges.

ACOLYTE DETAILS

Base: Retributor Armour.
Shade: Agrax Earthshade Gloss.
Highlight: Stormhost Silver.

Base: Leadbelcher.
Shade: Drakenhof Nightshade.
Highlight: Stormhost Silver.

Base: Caliban Green.
Highlight: Warpstone Glow, Moot Green.

Base: Kabalite Green.
Highlight: Sybarite Green, Moot Green.

TZEENTCHIAN ARMOUR

Base: Temple Guard Blue.
Recess Shade: 1:2 mix of Akhelian Green and Contrast Medium.
Highlight: Fenrisian Grey.

Base: Warpstone Glow.
Recess Shade: Ork Flesh.
Highlight: Moot Green. Take care to highlight alongside the shade.

Base: Incubi Darkness.
Highlight: Kabalite Green, Sybarite Green.

Base: Grey Seer.
Recess Shade: Apothecary White.
Highlight: White Scar.

TZEENTCHIAN BASING

Base with Leadbelcher and apply Gore-grunta Fur in a random pattern. Once dry, apply one thick coat of Mordant Earth. Drybrush with Dark Reaper and Russ Grey.

Base with Temple Guard Blue and apply some random patches of Talassar Blue. Once dry, apply one thick coat of Mordant Earth. Drybrush with Dawnstone and Administratum Grey.

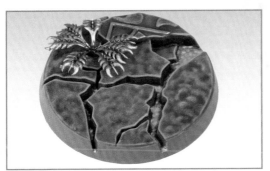 

For the river of metal in the cracks, base with Leadbelcher, layer with Stormhost Silver and apply Talassar Blue to the river's edges. Paint the Barbed Bracken in the same way as the Tzaangor weapons.

Base with Astrogranite and shade with Nuln Oil. Drybrush with Dawnstone and Administratum Grey. Paint the rocks in the same way as the Acolyte weapons and paint the gold sections in the same way as their masks.

DISCIPLES OF TZEENTCH

This battletome contains all of the rules you need to field your Tzeentch miniatures on the battlefields of the Mortal Realms, from a host of exciting allegiance abilities to a range of warscrolls and warscroll battalions. The rules are split into the following sections:

ALLEGIANCE ABILITIES

This section describes the allegiance abilities available to a Tzeentch army. The rules for using allegiance abilities can be found in the *Warhammer Age of Sigmar Core Book*.

BATTLE TRAITS

Abilities available to every unit in a Tzeentch army (pg 69-71).

COMMAND TRAITS

Abilities available to the general of a Tzeentch army if it is a **Hero** (pg 72-73).

ARTEFACTS OF POWER

Artefacts available to **Heroes** in a Tzeentch army (pg 74-75).

SPELL LORES

Spells available to **Wizards** in a Tzeentch army (pg 76-77).

CHANGE COVENS

Abilities for six of the mightiest convocations and cults (pg 78-83). These rules can be used by units in a Tzeentch army that have been given the appropriate keyword (see the Change Covens battle trait, opposite).

BATTLEPLAN

This section includes a new narrative battleplan that can be played with a Tzeentch army (pg 84-85).

PATH TO GLORY

This section contains rules for using your Tzeentch collection in Path to Glory campaigns (pg 86-89).

WARSCROLLS

This section includes all of the warscrolls you will need to play games of Warhammer Age of Sigmar with your Tzeentch miniatures. There are three types of warscroll included in this section:

WARSCROLL BATTALIONS

These are formations made up of several Tzeentch units that combine their strengths to gain powerful new abilities (pg 90-97).

WARSCROLLS

A warscroll for each unit is included here. The rules for using a Tzeentch unit, along with its characteristics and abilities, are detailed on its warscroll (pg 98-116).

ENDLESS SPELL WARSCROLLS

There are three endless spell warscrolls that detail the rules for unique and powerful spells that can be summoned by **Tzeentch Wizards** (pg 117-118).

The rules for playing games with endless spells can be found in the *Warhammer Age of Sigmar Core Book* and in *Warhammer Age of Sigmar: Malign Sorcery*.

PITCHED BATTLE PROFILES

This section contains Pitched Battle profiles for the units, warscroll battalions and endless spells in this book (pg 119-120).

ALLIES

This section has a list of the allies a Tzeentch army can include (pg 120).

ALLEGIANCE ABILITIES
BATTLE TRAITS

THE FLOW OF CHANGE

MASTERS OF DESTINY

To serve the Changer of the Ways is to instinctively understand the ebb and flow of future events and be able to manipulate their potential to the fullest.

After armies have been set up but before the first battle round begins, roll 9 dice and put them to one side. These are your Destiny Dice. Destiny Dice can be used during the battle to change the results of different dice rolls.

The number of Destiny Dice you have at any time must never exceed 9.

Designer's Note: *It is recommended that you represent your Destiny Dice using different-coloured and/or different-sized D6s to prevent confusion and easily keep track of their results in your games.*

Instead of making one of the rolls from the list below for a friendly **Tzeentch** unit, you can spend one or more of your Destiny Dice. The result of the roll you would have made is replaced with the value on the Destiny Dice you spent. For example, instead of rolling a dice to see how far a **Tzeentch** unit would run in the movement phase, you could spend a Destiny Dice to determine the distance. If you spent a Destiny Dice with a value of 5, the unit would run 5".

Destiny Dice can be spent in place of the following dice rolls:

- Casting rolls
- Unbinding rolls
- Dispelling rolls
- Run rolls
- Charge rolls
- Hit rolls
- Wound rolls
- Save rolls
- Any roll that determines the Damage characteristic of a missile or melee weapon
- Battleshock tests

Note that each Destiny Dice spent only allows you to replace a single dice roll. If you want to replace a 2D6 roll (such as a casting roll or charge roll), you must spend 2 Destiny Dice. In addition, any rolls that have been replaced count as unmodified rolls and cannot be re-rolled or modified further.

LOCUS OF CHANGE

The miasma of instability that follows the minions of the Great Conspirator can send even the most focused warriors insane, the deceit of their own eyes rendering any martial skill useless.

Subtract 1 from hit rolls for attacks made with melee weapons that target friendly **Tzeentch Daemon** units that are wholly within 12" of a friendly **Tzeentch Daemon Hero**.

CHANGE COVENS

The legions at Tzeentch's disposal are limitless. Daemons spill forth from the Crystal Labyrinth and appear as if from the aether to do the bidding of their master. Cults of Arcanites gather in secret and conspire to bring mighty cities to their knees. Where there is life, it is certain that Tzeentch will be at play, poring over the fine details and patterns of civilisations, ready to hatch a diabolical scheme and command his followers to carry out his ever-changing plans.

When you choose an Tzeentch army, you can give it a Change Coven keyword from the list below. All **Tzeentch** units in your army gain that keyword, and you can use the extra abilities listed for that Change Coven on the page indicated.

- **Eternal Conflagration** (pg 78)
- **Hosts Duplicitous** (pg 79)
- **Hosts Arcanum** (pg 80)
- **Cult of the Transient Form** (pg 81)
- **Pyrofane Cult** (pg 82)
- **Guild of Summoners** (pg 83)

If a model already has a Change Coven keyword on its warscroll, it cannot gain another one. This does not preclude you from including the unit in your army.

FROM THE CRYSTAL LABYRINTH

SUMMON DAEMONS OF TZEENTCH

The machinations of Tzeentch are unimaginably complex. To challenge the fractal plans of the Architect of Fate is to stand before the folding of reality and face strange daemons born from chaotic sorcery itself.

You can summon units of **TZEENTCH DAEMONS** to the battlefield if you collect enough Fate Points. Each time a casting roll (made by friend or foe) is successful and the spell is not unbound, you receive 1 Fate Point.

Once per turn, at the end of your movement phase, you can spend Fate Points to summon 1 unit from the list opposite to the battlefield and add it to your army.

Each unit you summon costs a number of Fate Points as shown on the list, and you can only summon a unit if you have enough Fate Points to do so.

Summoned units must be set up wholly within 12" of a friendly **TZEENTCH HERO** and more than 9" from any enemy units. Immediately after you have set up the summoned unit, subtract its cost from the total number of Fate Points you have.

DISCIPLES OF TZEENTCH UNIT	FATE POINT COST
1 Lord of Change	30
1 Fateskimmer, Herald of Tzeentch on Burning Chariot	24
10 Pink Horrors of Tzeentch	20
1 Burning Chariot of Tzeentch	18
3 Flamers of Tzeentch	18
1 Changecaster, Herald of Tzeentch	12
1 Exalted Flamer of Tzeentch	12
1 Fluxmaster, Herald of Tzeentch on Disc	12
10 Blue Horrors of Tzeentch	10
10 Brimstone Horrors of Tzeentch	10
3 Screamers of Tzeentch	10

AGENDAS OF ANARCHY

Should followers of Tzeentch adhere to the sacred number 9, whether through rituals or great feats in battle, the Master of Fate will bless his children with bounties that propel them to greater power.

At the start of your hero phase, you can say that your army intends to complete one of the following agendas before the start of your next hero phase. You must tell your opponent which agenda you intend to complete, and you cannot complete the same agenda more than once per battle.

If a friendly **Tzeentch** unit completes one of the following agendas during a battle, that unit gains that agenda's ability for the rest of the battle.

Friendly **Tzeentch** units that complete more than one agenda must choose which ability they wish to keep; any other abilities gained through this battle trait are lost.

Mass Conjuration:

Tzeentch acknowledges his cult's devotion and grants them increased mastery of their spell lore.

Agenda: Pick 1 friendly **Tzeentch Wizard**. If that **Wizard** successfully casts 2 spells and/or endless spells in that hero phase with an unmodified casting roll of 9+ and neither spell or endless spell is unbound, this agenda is completed.

Ability: Add 1 to casting rolls for the **Tzeentch Wizard** that completed this agenda.

Ninefold Dismantlement:

Offerings to the Changer of Ways are always welcome, but slaying his enemies in sacred numbers is greatly rewarded.

Agenda: Pick 1 enemy unit on the battlefield that has 9 or more models. If that unit is destroyed before the end of that turn, this agenda is completed.

Ability: Add 1 to hit rolls for attacks made with melee weapons by the friendly **Tzeentch** unit that destroyed that unit to complete this agenda.

Overthrow Leaders:

By claiming the heads of enemy champions and mighty beasts, Tzeentch's followers can earn enough favour to be blessed with the resilience to fight another day.

Agenda: Pick 1 enemy **Hero** or **Monster** on the battlefield with a Wounds characteristic of 9 or more. If that **Hero** or **Monster** is slain before the end of that turn, this agenda is completed.

Ability: Add 1 to save rolls for attacks that target the friendly **Tzeentch** unit that destroyed that **Hero** or **Monster** to complete this agenda.

Reckless Abandon:

Cabals eager to show their devotion to their god are given renewed vigour to unleash upon their enemies.

Agenda: At the start of your charge phase, pick 1 friendly **Tzeentch** unit that is 9" or more from any enemy units. If that unit ends a charge move in that charge phase within ½" of an enemy model, this agenda is completed.

Ability: Add 1 to the Attacks characteristic of melee weapons used by the **Tzeentch** unit that completed this agenda if that unit made a charge move in the same turn.

Tides of Anarchy:

Expanding the domain of their master is of critical value to the Disciples of Tzeentch, and any who uproot his enemies are reinforced in order to hold his newly claimed land.

Agenda: If a friendly **Tzeentch** unit that has 9 or more models gains control of an objective that was controlled by your opponent at the start of your hero phase, this agenda is completed (the friendly **Tzeentch** unit must have 9 or more models when it gains control of the objective).

Ability: Each **Tzeentch** model in the unit that completed this agenda counts as 2 models instead of 1 when determining control of that objective.

COMMAND TRAITS

TZEENTCH ARCANITES

Tzeentch Arcanite Hero generals only.

D6 Command Trait

1 **Arch-sorcerer:** *This disciple is driven by an obsession to obtain as much of Tzeentch's wisdom as possible.*

This general knows 2 extra spells from the Lore of Fate (pg 76).

2 **Nexus of Fate:** *This general manipulates what mortals consider 'destiny' as if it were a puppet.*

At the start of your hero phase, if this general is on the battlefield, you can roll a dice. If you do so, you can replace one of your Destiny Dice with that roll.

3 **Magical Supremacy:** *This sorcerer drills their execution of the arcane as a warrior would their swordsmanship.*

Add 12" to the range within which this general can attempt to unbind spells and dispel endless spells.

4 **Boundless Mutation:** *The flow of change runs through this disciple, curing any ailment or injury through rapid shifts in their form.*

At the start of your hero phase, if this general is on the battlefield, you can roll a dice. If you do so, on a 2+, you can heal D3 wounds allocated to this general.

5 **Cult Demagogue:** *This cabalist's resounding prayers draw the gaze of his master's minions quicker than most.*

If a casting roll for this general is a double, the casting attempt is automatically successful (regardless of the result). In addition, if the spell is not unbound, you receive 2 Fate Points instead of 1.

6 **Arcane Sacrifice:** *Blood rituals are rare amongst Tzeentch's Arcanites – but not unheard of.*

At the start of your hero phase, you can inflict 1 mortal wound on a friendly **Tzeentch** unit within 3" of this general. If you do so, until the end of that phase, add 9" to the range of any spell successfully cast by this general.

TZEENTCH MORTALS

Tzeentch Mortal Hero generals only.

D3 Command Trait

1 **Nexus of Fate:** *This general manipulates what mortals consider 'destiny' as if it were a puppet.*

At the start of your hero phase, if this general is on the battlefield, you can roll a dice. If you do so, you can replace one of your Destiny Dice with that roll.

2 **Soul Burn:** *The slightest contact with this champion's blade can blight the very fabric of the victim's body.*

If the unmodified hit roll for an attack made with a melee weapon by this general is 6, that attack inflicts 1 mortal wound on the target in addition to any normal damage.

3 **Illusionist:** *This warrior uses misdirection and cunning to render his enemies clueless.*

Subtract 1 from hit rolls for attacks that target this general.

TZEENTCH DAEMONS
Tzeentch Daemon Hero generals only.

D6	Command Trait

1 Arch-sorcerer: *This disciple is driven by an obsession to obtain as much of Tzeentch's wisdom as possible.*

This general knows 2 extra spells from the Lore of Change (pg 77).

2 Nexus of Fate: *This general manipulates what mortals consider 'destiny' as if it were a puppet.*

At the start of your hero phase, if this general is on the battlefield, you can roll a dice. If you do so, you can replace one of your Destiny Dice with that roll.

3 Magical Supremacy: *This sorcerer drills their execution of the arcane as a warrior would their swordsmanship.*

Add 12" to the range within which this general can attempt to unbind spells and dispel endless spells.

4 Daemonspark: *This crude object is fused with the daemon's chest and acts as a beacon to which its master's minions flock.*

Once per battle, in your hero phase, you can say that this general will use their Daemonspark. If you do so, you immediately gain 3 Fate Points.

5 Incorporeal Form: *This daemon can transform into a translucent state when malevolent sorcery draws near.*

Each time this general is affected by a spell or endless spell, you can roll a dice. On a 5+, ignore the effects of that spell or endless spell on this general.

6 Aether-tether: *This daemon phases in and out of the physical plane, making it almost impossible to attack.*

Add 1 to save rolls for attacks that target this general.

ARTEFACTS OF POWER

FATED ARTEFACTS

Tzeentch Mortal Heroes only.

D6 **Artefact of Power**

1 **Wicked Shard:** *Empowered by the bearer's sorcerous might, this blade is anathema to life.*

Pick 1 of the bearer's melee weapons. You can re-roll wound rolls for attacks made with that weapon.

2 **Changeblade:** *To fall to this blade is to be transmuted into a writhing mass of flesh and tentacles.*

Pick 1 of the bearer's melee weapons. Each time an enemy **Hero** is slain by attacks made with that weapon, after all of the bearer's attacks have been resolved and before removing the slain model, you can add 1 **Tzeentch Chaos Spawn** to your army. Set up the **Tzeentch Chaos Spawn** within 1" of the slain **Hero**.

3 **Nexus Staff:** *Those slain by this cursed stave have their soul-stuff torn from their bodies to fuel a terrible enchantment upon their former brothers in arms.*

Once per battle, in your hero phase, you can pick 1 endless spell within 9" of the bearer. If you do so, that endless spell is dispelled.

4 **Timeslip Pendant:** *Time is a mutable concept to the bearer of this amulet.*

Once per battle, at the end of the combat phase, you can say that the bearer will enter a timeslip. If you do so, the bearer can fight for a second time.

5 **Daemonheart:** *Through a dark ritual, the heart of a daemon dwells within the bearer's chest, where its dread power can be unleashed to greatly augment the strength of its host.*

Once per battle, at the start of the combat phase, before the players pick any units to fight, you can say the bearer will unleash the power of their Daemonheart. If you do so, pick 1 enemy unit within 1" of the bearer. That unit suffers 3 mortal wounds.

6 **Paradoxical Shield:** *This shield flickers simultaneously between the physical and ethereal planes.*

Add 2 to save rolls for attacks that target the bearer. However, you must re-roll any successful save rolls made for the bearer.

TREASURES OF THE CULTS

Tzeentch Arcanite Heroes only.

D3 **Artefact of Power**

1 **Ambition's End:** *Many a sorcerer's quest to master the magical arts has ended upon this weapon's blade, for it spills not only blood but knowledge itself.*

Once per battle, at the start of your hero phase, you can pick 1 enemy **Wizard** within 1" of the bearer. That **Wizard** suffers D3 mortal wounds. In addition, that **Wizard** cannot attempt to unbind any spells until your next hero phase.

2 **Secret-eater:** *Should this weapon slay one touched by fate, its bearer inherits a measure of their destiny.*

Pick 1 of the bearer's weapons. If the unmodified hit roll for an attack made with that weapon is 6, you can roll a dice and add it to your Destiny Dice.

3 **Spiteful Shield:** *This shield exemplifies Tzeentch's predilection for cruel twists of fate.*

If the unmodified save roll for an attack made with a melee weapon that targets the bearer is 6, the attacking unit suffers 2 mortal wounds after all of its attacks have been resolved.

DAEMONIC WEAPONS
Tzeentch Daemon Heroes only.

D6 Artefact of Power

1 Warpfire Blade: *The flames that flicker around this daemon's blade can ignite the soul of its victim.*

Pick 1 of the bearer's melee weapons. If the unmodified hit roll for an attack made with that weapon is 6, that attack inflicts 2 mortal wounds on the target in addition to any normal damage.

2 Sentient Weapons: *This daemon's armaments seem to be guided by their own unerring will.*

If the unmodified hit roll for an attack made with a melee weapon by the bearer is 6, and the target bears an artefact of power, the target no longer bears that artefact of power (if a weapon was picked when the artefact of power was selected, that weapon reverts to normal).

3 Blade of Fate: *This daemon's blade will serve its master well – if they can tame the vagaries of fate.*

Pick 1 of the bearer's melee weapons. Once per battle, if the unmodified hit roll for an attack made with that weapon is 6, you can replace one of your Destiny Dice with that roll.

4 Souleater: *This evil blade grows stronger as it gluts itself upon souls of sufficient worth.*

Pick 1 of the bearer's melee weapons. If any enemy **Heroes** are slain by attacks made with that weapon, after all of the bearer's attacks have been resolved, add 1 to that weapon's Attacks characteristic for the rest of the battle.

5 Phantasmal Weapons: *This daemon's strikes can pass through armour to cleave the flesh beneath.*

Improve the Rend characteristic of the bearer's melee weapons by 1.

6 Pyrofyre Stave: *This ornate staff is wreathed in flickering warpflame, and any touched by the aetheric fire channelled through it are purged of any arcane energy they hold.*

Pick 1 of the bearer's melee weapons. If any wounds inflicted by that weapon are allocated to an enemy **Wizard** and that model is not slain, that **Wizard** cannot unbind spells for the rest of the battle.

DAEMONIC POWERS
Tzeentch Daemon Heroes only.

D3 Artefact of Power

1 Aura of Mutability: *Even the slightest injury serves as an opportunity for bountiful change when in close proximity to this daemon.*

Add 1 to wound rolls for attacks made by friendly **Tzeentch Daemon** units that are wholly within 9" of the bearer.

2 Wellspring of Arcane Might: *This daemon is a living font of sorcerous energy, upon which his minions can draw to fuel their own spells.*

You can re-roll casting and unbinding rolls for the bearer.

3 Aspect of Tzeentch: *To know even a fraction of the Architect of Fate's power is to know the boundless possibilities of destiny and how best to manipulate it.*

If the bearer is on the battlefield, roll a dice each time you spend a Destiny Dice. On a 5+, you can roll a dice and add it to your Destiny Dice.

SPELL LORES

You can choose or roll for one spell from one of the following tables for each **TZEENTCH WIZARD HERO** in a Tzeentch army.

LORE OF FATE
TZEENTCH ARCANITE WIZARDS and **TZEENTCH MORTAL WIZARDS** only.

D6 Spell

1 Bolt of Tzeentch: *This spell manifests as a prismatic beam of raw magic that tears its victims apart in a display of multispectral colour.*

Bolt of Tzeentch has a casting value of 7. If successfully cast, pick 1 enemy unit within 18" of the caster and visible to them. That unit suffers D6 mortal wounds. This spell cannot be cast more than once per turn, even though it appears in both the Lore of Fate and the Lore of Change.

2 Arcane Suggestion: *Overwhelming reason with magical force of will, the sorcerer's victims are reduced to little more than puppets on a string.*

Arcane Suggestion has a casting value of 8. If successfully cast, pick 1 enemy unit within 18" of the caster that is visible to them and pick one of the following effects:

It's Hopeless: That unit suffers D3 mortal wounds.

Drop Your Weapons: Subtract 1 from hit and wound rolls for attacks made by that unit until your next hero phase.

Kneel: Subtract 1 from save rolls for attacks that target that unit until your next hero phase.

3 Glimpse the Future: *By focusing on the skeins of potential fates, the sorcerer can glean hints as to future events in time to manipulate them to their advantage.*

Glimpse the Future has a casting value of 7. If successfully cast, you can roll a dice and add it to your Destiny Dice.

4 Shield of Fate: *There is little better protection than to be guided by destiny itself, defended by the very hand of fate.*

Shield of Fate has a casting value of 6. If successfully cast, pick 1 friendly **TZEENTCH** unit wholly within 18" of the caster and visible to them. Until the start of your next hero phase, that unit gains one of the following effects based on the number of your remaining Destiny Dice:

1-3 You can re-roll save rolls of 1 for attacks that target that unit.

4-6 You can re-roll save rolls for attacks that target that unit.

7-9 You can roll a dice each time that unit is affected by a spell or endless spell. On a 4+, ignore the effects of that spell or endless spell on that unit. In addition, you can re-roll save rolls for attacks that target that unit.

5 Infusion Arcanum: *The sorcerer's body becomes saturated with death-dealing energies, transforming even the frailest warlock into a truly formidable adversary.*

Infusion Arcanum has a casting value of 5. If successfully cast, add 1 to hit and wound rolls for attacks made by the caster until your next hero phase.

6 Treacherous Bond: *By creating a psycho-conductive link, the sorcerer can siphon the worst of any harm that befalls them to allies nearby.*

Treacherous Bond has a casting value of 5. If successfully cast, pick 1 friendly **TZEENTCH MORTAL** unit wholly within 9" of the caster and visible to them. Until your next hero phase, roll a dice before you allocate any wounds or mortal wounds to the caster. On a 3+, you must allocate those wounds or mortal wounds to that friendly unit instead.

LORE OF CHANGE
Tzeentch Daemon Wizards only.

D6 Spell

1 Bolt of Tzeentch: *This spell manifests as a prismatic beam of raw magic that tears its victims apart in a display of multispectral colour.*

Bolt of Tzeentch has a casting value of 7. If successfully cast, pick 1 enemy unit within 18" of the caster and visible to them. That unit suffers D6 mortal wounds. This spell cannot be cast more than once per turn, even though it appears in both the Lore of Change and the Lore of Fate.

2 Treason of Tzeentch: *Tzeentch delights in sowing treachery and deceit, and many of his daemonic sorcerers can channel this aspect of their master's power to set brother upon brother.*

Treason of Tzeentch has a casting value of 5. If successfully cast, pick 1 enemy unit within 18" of the caster and visible to them. Roll a number of dice equal to the number of models in that unit. For each 6, that unit suffers 1 mortal wound. If any models from that unit are slain by this spell, subtract 1 from hit rolls for attacks made by that unit until your next hero phase.

3 Arcane Transformation: *This daemon can call upon its master to grant the blessing of mutation.*

Arcane Transformation has a casting value of 6. If successfully cast, pick 1 friendly **Tzeentch Hero** wholly within 18" of the caster and visible to them. Until your next hero phase, you can either add 1 to that **Hero**'s Move and Bravery characteristics or add 1 to the Attacks characteristic of one of that **Hero**'s melee weapons.

4 Unchecked Mutation: *Those touched by this mutagenic spell either evolve so fast that their bodies are torn apart or suffer spontaneous hyper-devolution into a mass of primordial ooze.*

Unchecked Mutation has a casting value of 6. If successfully cast, pick 1 enemy unit within 18" of the caster and visible to them. That unit suffers D3 mortal wounds. If any models from that unit are slain by this spell, you can roll a dice. On a 3+, that unit suffers an additional D3 mortal wounds and this spell ends.

5 Fold Reality: *This spell holds the power to undo and remake existence at will, though doing so is never without its risks…*

Fold Reality has a casting value of 7. If successfully cast, pick 1 friendly **Tzeentch Daemon** unit wholly within 18" of the caster and visible to them, and roll a dice. On a 1, that unit is destroyed. On a 2+, you can return a number of slain models equal to that roll to that unit. Set up the models one at a time within 1" of a model from that unit that has not been returned in that phase. The models can only be set up within 3" of an enemy unit if the friendly unit was within 3" of that enemy unit before any models were returned.

6 Tzeentch's Firestorm: *An apocalyptic inferno of raging warpflame surges from the daemon's hands to engulf its victims in a fiery maelstrom.*

Tzeentch's Firestorm has a casting value of 9. If successfully cast, pick 1 enemy unit within 18" of the caster that is visible to them, and roll 9 dice. For each 6, that unit suffers D3 mortal wounds.

THE ETERNAL CONFLAGRATION

Those who see the flaming triskele of the Eternal Conflagration on the field of war have but one fate ahead of them – to be swathed in mutating warpflame. The disciples of this host revel in the awful changes such magical fire brings, cackling with glee as their enemies are mutated and twisted into horrific new forms even as they burn alive.

All will burn when the hosts of the Eternal Conflagration arrive on the battlefield. Here is no subterfuge or subtlety, for it is this convocation that Tzeentch sends forth when he deems it time to scour the foe and blast them with unnatural flames. The Flamers of the Eternal Conflagration burn brightest of all, lighting the horizon like a psychedelic sun. The Lord of Change that commands this convocation holds the title of Radiant Lord, and it is tasked with bringing fiery annihilation to those who would thwart the plans of Tzeentch. To touch this daemon or its favoured agents is to burn, for it does not take kindly to physical assault. At least such brave souls have a quick death. Sooner or later, all must be consumed by the flames of change.

Nothing pleases the Eternal Conflagration more than the spectacle of mutating fire playing across their victims – not so much burning as reshaping, flowing and killing with sheer unbound flux. Even supernatural adversaries cannot withstand their forms going through a dozen changes every second. Armour provides little defence; a duardin-crafted breastplate that could turn aside a ballista's bolt is suddenly transmuted to a sloughing mass of frogspawn, a puff of sentient steam or a clawing thicket of thorned fingernails that rip and tear even as the fire burns on. As flesh distends, twists and distorts into hideous new shapes, the few yet to be touched by the flames flee in panic and disarray.

ABILITIES

Twisters of Materiality: *The volatile nature of Eternal Conflagration warpflame cares not for reinforced bulwarks or master craftsmanship.*

Improve the Rend characteristic of friendly **ETERNAL CONFLAGRATION** units' Warpflame, Billowing Warpflame and Magical Flames missile weapons by 1.

COMMAND ABILITY

Infernos of Mutation: *The dazzling flares of wyrdflame conjured by these daemons leave foes horrified by the grotesque changes they bring.*

You can use this command ability in the shooting phase. If you do so, pick 1 friendly **ETERNAL CONFLAGRATION DAEMON** unit wholly within 12" of a friendly **ETERNAL CONFLAGRATION DAEMON HERO**. If the unmodified hit roll for any attack made by that unit's Warpflame, Billowing Warpflame or Magical Flames missile weapons is 6, subtract 2 from the Bravery characteristic of the target unit until the end of that battle round. A unit cannot benefit from this command ability more than once per turn.

COMMAND TRAIT

An **ETERNAL CONFLAGRATION** general must have this command trait instead of one listed on pages 72-73.

Coruscating Flames: *As the Eternal Conflagration bound and cavort across the battlefield, their fires burn ever brighter, dazzling their foes.*

Subtract 1 from hit rolls for attacks made with missile weapons that target friendly **ETERNAL CONFLAGRATION DAEMON** units wholly within 12" of this general.

ARTEFACT OF POWER

The first **ETERNAL CONFLAGRATION HERO** to receive an artefact of power must be given the Shroud of Warpflame.

Shroud of Warpflame: *Cloaked in an unending veil of unnatural fire, the bearer can set alight any who manage to land a strike.*

Roll a dice each time you allocate a wound or mortal wound inflicted by a melee weapon to the bearer. On a 3+, the attacking unit suffers 1 mortal wound.

THE HOSTS DUPLICITOUS

The eaters of truth, the bringers of madness, the lords of confusion: all these names and more describe the Hosts Duplicitous. To fight them is to battle insanity – and, all too often, to discover that the battle has already been lost before the first blow is struck. Those who duel the masters of this host will find they strike only at thin air.

The daemons of the Hosts Duplicitous are masters of illusion and deception. Tzeentch sends forth this convocation's hosts on any number of covert actions, such as effecting secret regime changes or stealthily infiltrating well-guarded places of power, but this is only a prelude to the grand denouement to come. On the day of battle, the Hosts Duplicitous appear as if from nowhere. Columns of refugees or feeble-looking scribes reveal themselves as cultists and warrior mages, springing their ambush on their reeling enemies. Daemons leap from fiery portals; bolts of magic sear all around. Once the first blow is struck, these disciples are well prepared to capitalise, for their deceit knows no bounds. They use spell-generated mirages to bolster their ranks, holding back the enemy's counter-assaults and allowing their true forces to strike while their foes waste their efforts on mere hallucinations.

The Lord of Change that leads the Hosts Duplicitous holds the sinister title of Phantom Lord; like all those who bear its mark, it blurs through reality as it moves, existing in two places at once yet being fully corporeal in neither. It and its minions are expert spellcasters, for Tzeentch is generous to those who lie, manipulate and deceive as a way of life. It is said that those who fight the Hosts Duplicitous must fight not only Tzeentch's disciples but also their own senses. Those without the wit to tell mirage from truth will pay for their lack of insight with their lives.

ABILITIES

Ranks of Mischievous Mirages: *Warriors that face the Hosts Duplicitous in battle find themselves tangled in ranks of mere phantasms, rendering them exhausted and confused with little chance of escape.*

Enemy units within 3" of a **Hosts Duplicitous** unit cannot retreat.

COMMAND ABILITY

Impossible to Anticipate: *Some of the many illusions set upon the foe by the Hosts Duplicitous contain denser manifestations of Tzeentch's power, summoning additional daemons should they be destroyed.*

You can use this command ability once per battle, immediately after a friendly **Hosts Duplicitous Horrors of Tzeentch** unit is destroyed. If you do so, roll a dice. On a 5+, a new unit identical to the one that was destroyed is added to your army. Set up the new unit wholly within 12" of a friendly **Hosts Duplicitous Hero** and more than 9" from any enemy units.

COMMAND TRAIT

A **Hosts Duplicitous** general must have this command trait instead of one listed on pages 72-73.

Will of the Phantom Lord: *This general extends his connection with Tzeentch to his loyal sorcerers.*

You can re-roll casting and unbinding rolls for friendly **Hosts Duplicitous Daemon Wizards** while they are wholly within 9" of this general.

ARTEFACT OF POWER

The first **Hosts Duplicitous Hero** to receive an artefact of power must be given the Brand of the Split Daemon.

Brand of the Split Daemon: *This twisting, two-headed mark represents the bearer's mastery of deception, tricking enemies into attacking decoys of itself before striking from unprotected angles.*

Add 1 to save rolls for attacks that target the bearer.

THE HOSTS ARCANUM

The Hosts Arcanum are considered pre-eminent spellcasters in a realm of daemons formed of pure magic. Though they prefer to pore over forbidden knowledge, they are frighteningly powerful when roused to battle, the sheer potency of their spells attracting shoals of Screamers that dive down to lacerate and gnaw the foe.

The Hosts Arcanum are unusual amongst the daemons of the Realm of Chaos, for they are usually content to dwell in the endless libraries and scholariums of the Crystal Labyrinth, amassing and analysing every spell cast in every reality they can penetrate. They love nothing more than poring over tomes, grimoires and parchments, as well as stranger devices such as crystal wafers, enigma boxes and repositories of information that, although no bigger than a human thumb, each contain more knowledge than the Great Library of Elixia. When Tzeentch requires them to enter reality on a war footing, they resent every moment spent away from their precious knowledge-hoards, and they employ the fastest daemons and most spectacular spells they can muster in order to cut short the ordeal. The only silver lining is that the mortal races are dabblers in the arcane, and in their short-lived ingenuity, these curious fools invent new spells and rites that the Hosts Arcanum can capture even as they are cast, taking that power for themselves and recording it upon their return to the Crystal Labyrinth.

The concentration of spells and unnatural energies that typifies a Hosts Arcanum force sees the skies fill with Screamers, for the sky-sharks are drawn to magic in all its forms. Though the convocation is beset by shoals of these daemons and their distracting screeching, they are a potent asset in battle, providing fodder for the enemy's guns and blades as the spellcasters weave their magic.

ABILITIES

Thieves of All Things Arcane: *Driven by an unquenchable thirst for knowledge, there is no sorcery the Hosts Arcanum do not seek to take for their own.*

Once per turn, in the first, third and fifth battle rounds, when a friendly **HOSTS ARCANUM WIZARD** attempts to unbind a spell, the spell is automatically unbound (do not roll 2D6).

COMMAND ABILITY

Entourage of Sky-sharks: *The numberless Screamers of the Hosts Arcanum include some of the most tenacious of Tzeentch's legions.*

You can use this command ability in your hero phase. If you do so, pick 1 friendly **HOSTS ARCANUM SCREAMERS OF TZEENTCH** unit wholly within 12" of a friendly **HOSTS ARCANUM HERO**. Until your next hero phase, add 1 to save rolls for attacks that target that unit. In addition, until your next hero phase, improve the Rend characteristic of that unit's Lamprey Bite by 1. A unit cannot benefit from the effects of this ability more than once per turn.

COMMAND TRAIT

A **HOSTS ARCANUM** general must have this command trait instead of one listed on pages 72-73.

Spell Hunters: *The flying beasts of this convocation set off to find their quarry long before a battle commences.*

After armies have been set up but before the first battle round begins, D3 friendly **HOSTS ARCANUM** units that can fly can move up to 6".

ARTEFACT OF POWER

The first **HOSTS ARCANUM HERO** to receive an artefact of power must be given the Fanged Circlet.

The Fanged Circlet: *Said to be made from the fangs of the feared Screamers of Idano, this circlet's engraved teeth glow as it calls its kin to the battlefield.*

Once per battle, at the start of your hero phase, you can add 1 unit of 6 **SCREAMERS OF TZEENTCH** to your army. Set up the unit wholly within 9" of the bearer and more than 9" away from any enemy units.

THE CULT OF THE TRANSIENT FORM

The Cult of the Transient Form is known for its hosts of avian beastmen, warriors whose natural arrogance is justified by their skill at arms. Many of these were once men and women, for the acolytes of this cult want nothing more than to transform into Tzaangors and be closer to their god – even in the midst of a raging battle…

None embrace the power of change as zealously as the Cult of the Transient Form. To them, the splitting of Tzeentch's Horrors into lesser daemons demonstrates that, with enough sacrifice, a new form can be taken in which to serve the Great Mutator. Many of its human members actively seek to be transformed into Tzaangors, whom they regard as closer to Tzeentch in form and spirit, and the prideful gor-kin are only too happy to indulge them. Death is seen not as the end for these fanatics but as the gateway to a glorious new beginning. Enemies are horrified as the corpses of slain cultists quiver and spasm, their flesh running like candle wax, before rising once more as shrieking Tzaangors – or something altogether more terrifying.

The leaders of the Cult have higher ambitions than simply becoming beastmen. They are happy to further such a transformation amongst their vassals, and will even make pacts with supernatural entities to ensure it happens, but for their own personal fate, nothing short of full daemonhood will suffice. They fool themselves into thinking they walk the Path to Glory as do any other scions of Chaos, but in truth, it is the act of change itself they crave, and they will never be happy wearing one single form. So does the scholar take the form of the Kairic Acolyte, then the Tzaangor, then perhaps the Daemon Prince or the Chaos Spawn. Any who stand in their way will soon find just how dangerous such maniacs can be…

ABILITIES
The Change-gift: *Acolytes from this cult fight to their last breath to prove themselves worthy of transcendence – and, just occasionally, earn that exact reward.*

Roll a dice each time a friendly **Cult of the Transient Form Kairic Acolyte** model is slain in the combat phase. On a 2-5, before removing that model from play, that model can fight. On a 6, before removing that model from play, you can add 1 **Tzaangor** model to an existing **Tzaangor** unit in your army. If you do so, set up that **Tzaangor** model within 1" of a friendly **Tzaangor** unit that is within 9" of the slain model. The model can only be set up within 3" of an enemy unit if the friendly **Tzaangor** unit was within 3" of that enemy unit before any models were added.

COMMAND ABILITY
Fate of Transmutation: *Champions of this cult manipulate the strands of destiny to propel their brothers into their revered form.*

You can use this command ability in your hero phase. If you do so, pick 1 **Cult of the Transient Form Kairic Acolyte** unit wholly within 12" of a friendly **Cult of the Transient Form Hero**. Until your next hero phase, each time a **Kairic Acolyte** model from that unit is slain, add 1 to the dice roll made for that unit's Change-gift ability.

COMMAND TRAIT
A **Cult of the Transient Form** general must have this command trait instead of one listed on pages 72-73.

Defiant in their Pursuit: *Nothing matters to this general and his cabal other than their transcendence.*

Add 2 to the Bravery characteristic of friendly **Cult of the Transient Form** units wholly within 12" of this general.

ARTEFACT OF POWER
The first **Cult of the Transient Form Hero** to receive an artefact of power must be given the Chaotica Amulet.

Chaotica Amulet: *Stolen from a rival sect, this amulet can give the bearer a second chance at ascension.*

Add 1 to the bearer's Wounds characteristic.

THE PYROFANE CULT

The sole agenda of the Pyrofane Cult is the utter immolation of the Mortal Realms. They wish to engulf Aqshy in warpfire, to melt Chamon, to burn away the mists of Shyish and to turn glorious Azyr to ash. The flames they send propagate fast, feeding on strife as true fire feeds on kindling. Some even walk as an inferno themselves.

The Pyrofane Cult revels in destruction. Their arcane pyrotechnics build upon themselves, gathering strength like an out-of-control wildfire. Each burning flame that they chant into existence sears with unnatural fury; unlike the wild energies of the Eternal Conflagration, these neither mutate nor bring sudden growth but instead incinerate, propagate and burn anew. The bolts of fire hurled by the Kairic Acolytes that form the massed ranks of this cult are great blazing sheets of flame that make it all but impossible to miss their targets entirely. Few enemies dare to confront such an inferno for long, as the air itself begins to smoulder and smoke. Even the act of drawing breath becomes next to impossible; those who inhale the fumes of the Pyrofane Cult's works will burn from within.

Tzeentch blesses those who bring the corrupting flames to his enemies, granting the Pyrofane Cult's sorcerers the ability to cast flickering chainfires that leap from foe to foe. When these leaders concentrate their efforts with those of their minions, fire builds upon fire, turning enemies to ash in a matter of moments. Those truly favoured by Tzeentch will be clad in living flame when in their full battle raiment: these sentient infernos burn up arrows and melt crossbow bolts before they can harm their master. Soon enough, the enemy will feel the kiss of that same fire. True glory comes only through fiery ruination, and the Pyrofane Cult are its masters.

ABILITIES
Arrows of Tzeentch: *To the Pyrofane Cult, immolation is the path to glory. Each bolt cast in Tzeentch's name falls upon the foe with burning devotion.*

Add 1 to hit rolls for attacks made with Sorcerous Bolts by friendly **PYROFANE CULT KAIRIC ACOLYTE** units. In addition, at the end of your shooting phase, roll a dice for each enemy unit that suffered any wounds inflicted by attacks made with Sorcerous Bolts by friendly **PYROFANE CULT** units in that phase. On a 5+, that unit suffers D3 mortal wounds.

COMMAND ABILITY
Immolate: *The champions of this cult exhort their brothers to unleash new volleys of searing bolts at the foe.*

You can use this command ability in your shooting phase. If you do so, pick 1 friendly **PYROFANE CULT KAIRIC ACOLYTE** unit wholly within 12" of a friendly **PYROFANE CULT HERO**. You can re-roll wound rolls for attacks made by that unit until the end of that phase.

COMMAND TRAIT
A **PYROFANE CULT** general must have this command trait instead of one listed on pages 72-73.

Shrouded in Unnatural Flame: *Such is the Pyrofane Cult's adoration of fire that their champions walk upon the battlefield in constantly conjured cloaks of warpflame, dazzling enemies and inspiring the faithful.*

Subtract 1 from hit rolls for attacks made with missile weapons that target this general.

ARTEFACT OF POWER
The first **PYROFANE CULT HERO** to receive an artefact of power must be given the Chainfire Amulet.

Chainfire Amulet: *The ever-burning blaze within this treasure fuels the bearer's conjurations of wyrdflame, transforming volleys of fiery bolts into raging wildfires.*

If the unmodified hit roll for an attack made with a missile weapon by the bearer is 6, that attack inflicts D3 mortal wounds on the target and the attack sequence ends (do not make a wound or save roll).

THE GUILD OF SUMMONERS

Secretive and sly, the Guild of Summoners specialises in the conjuration of daemons – Lords of Change above all. Their goal is to bring into being no fewer than nine of Tzeentch's greater daemons at once and, in doing so, achieve supremacy over reality. By the time they realise that they are the slaves and not the masters, it will be too late.

Known simply as the Guild amongst the conjurers that form its ranks, this Arcanite Cult gathers in secret rituals to share the dark arts of daemonology. Its members may begin their journey into madness through the summonation of small familiar daemons, perhaps in the forms of living books, long-legged fish or spiteful Brimstone Horrors, yet they all seek the same goal – to summon nine specific Lords of Change into reality. They come from all walks of life; peasants and kings stand shoulder to shoulder and refer to one another only by their guild-names, their identities always concealed by grotesque masks. In their fond imaginings, these aspirants believe that, once summoned, the greater daemons of Tzeentch will be bound to do their bidding, elevating them to new levels of wealth and status or even lending them supernatural powers.

The truth is that they already serve the group of nine Lords of Change known as the Exiled. These daemons have fallen into disgrace with Tzeentch and will only be able to earn his favour if they are all summoned in the same place at the same time by mortal agency. The great plan of the Guild nears completion. On several occasions, fuelled by the mayhem and sacrifice of open battle, they have summoned three, five, even seven Lords of Change to their service, but they have yet to bring all nine into being at once. With each year, their plans and skills become more refined. Surely it is only a matter of time…

ABILITIES
Scions of the Exiled: *In a supposedly ancient prophecy that led to the Guild's creation, the summoners must bind nine Lords of Change in order to ascend to true enlightenment. In reality, this will see their doom.*

If your army has the **GUILD OF SUMMONERS** keyword, your Fate Points can only be used to summon **LORD OF CHANGE** units. Instead of a Fate Point cost of 30, a **GUILD OF SUMMONERS LORD OF CHANGE** costs 9 Fate Points to summon the first time, 18 Fate Points the second time, and 30 Fate Points each time thereafter for the rest of the battle.

COMMAND ABILITY
Will of the Arcane Lords: *The Guild believes their cause is blessed by Tzeentch and do not question the flow of arcane energy bestowed upon their champions.*

You can use this command ability in your hero phase. If you do so, pick a friendly **GUILD OF SUMMONERS WIZARD** wholly within 9" of a friendly **GUILD OF SUMMONERS HERO** or wholly within 18" of a friendly **GUILD OF SUMMONERS HERO** that is a general. Add 1 to casting rolls for that **WIZARD** until the end of

that phase. A unit cannot benefit from this command ability more than once per turn.

COMMAND TRAIT
A **GUILD OF SUMMONERS** general must have this command trait instead of one listed on pages 72-73.

Prophet of the Ostensible: *This general blindly leads his guild through unrelenting devotion to Tzeentch.*

If this general is part of your army and on the battlefield at the start of your hero phase, roll a dice. On a 4+, you receive 1 extra command point.

ARTEFACT OF POWER
The first **GUILD OF SUMMONERS HERO** to receive an artefact of power must be given a Brimstone Familiar.

Brimstone Familiar: *A gift from one of the Exiled, this diminutive daemon inspires the brotherhood when uncertainty takes hold.*

Do not take battleshock tests for friendly **GUILD OF SUMMONERS** units while they are wholly within 12" of the bearer.

BATTLEPLAN
THE CONCEALED CULTIST

The rite of summonation is nearly complete! Some amongst those desperate to stop it believe that should it reach its conclusion, nine Lords of Change will manifest in reality and doom the lands to eternal servitude. Others believe it will conjure Vitrix, the Glass Cockatrice, a godbeast tainted by Tzeentch that will drink the rivers and turn the earth barren. Still more say that the rite will set loose a living tide of Brimstone Horrors numbering in the millions and wreath the nation in living fire. Whatever the truth – and the Disciples of Tzeentch are not swift to share it – it is sure to be disastrous.

The rite is being led by a Cult Leader, a warrior mage of impressive cunning who has concealed themselves with mirage and illusion – the better to guide the ritual to completion. Should their whereabouts be uncovered and should they be wounded unto death, or at least to the point that they can continue the rite no more, there is a hope that the great spell can be stopped. But should the Witch Seeker be confounded, this land will soon belong only to the Changer of the Ways…

THE ARMIES
Each player picks an army as described in the core rules. One player is the Tzeentch player. Their opponent is the Witch Seeker. The Tzeentch player must use a Tzeentch army.

SET-UP
The players alternate setting up units one at a time, starting with the Tzeentch player. Units must be set up wholly within their own territory, more than 12" from enemy territory. The territories are shown on the map.

The general of the Tzeentch army must be the Cult Leader and must be set up as a reserve unit. The Cult Leader cannot be set up on the battlefield until their hiding place has been revealed (see Ritual Sites).

Continue to set up units until both players have set up their armies. If one player finishes first, their opponent must set up the rest of the units in their army, one after another.

RITUAL SITES
The geomantic magic of the Mortal Realms concentrates in places of power and can be exploited by a gifted mage.

There are 4 points on the battlefield marked as ritual sites. At the start of the Witch Seeker's hero phase, 1 friendly **HERO** within 3" of a ritual site can search it to see if they can find the concealed Cult Leader.

To do so, roll a dice. On a 6, that ritual site is revealed to be the hiding place of the Cult Leader and all other ritual sites must be removed from the battlefield. Otherwise, the Cult Leader is not found and that ritual site must be removed from the battlefield.

If, at any point, 3 ritual sites have been searched and the Cult Leader has not been found, the last remaining ritual site is revealed to be the Cult Leader's hiding place.

If, at the start of the fifth battle round, the hiding place of the Cult Leader has still not been revealed, the players roll off (before any endless spells are moved). Starting with the player who won the roll-off, the players alternate removing

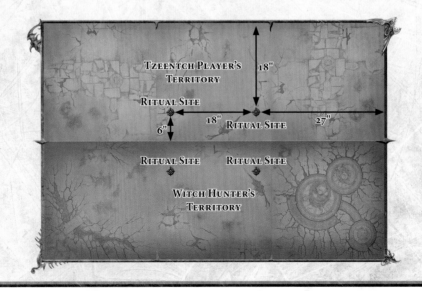

ritual sites from the battlefield, one at a time, until one remains. The remaining ritual site is revealed to be the Cult Leader's hiding place.

Once the hiding place of the Cult Leader has been revealed, the model must be set up within 9" of the ritual site. 2 units of 10 **Horrors of Tzeentch** are then immediately added to the Tzeentch player's army. These units must be set up wholly within 18" of the Cult Leader and more than 9" away from any enemy units.

BATTLE LENGTH

The battle lasts for 5 battle rounds.

GLORIOUS VICTORY

If the Cult Leader has not been slain when the battle ends, the Tzeentch player wins a **major victory**.

If the Cult Leader is slain before the end of the fifth battle round, the Witch Seeker wins a **major victory**.

PATH TO GLORY

Path to Glory campaigns centre around collecting and fighting a series of battles in the Mortal Realms. Players start off with a small warband. Over the course of several battles, each warband will gather more followers to join them in their quest for glory and renown.

In order to take part in a Path to Glory campaign, you will need two or more players. Each player will need a **Hero** to be their champion and must then create a warband to follow their champion into battle.

The players fight battles against each other using the warbands they have created. The results of these battles will gain their warbands glory. After battle, warbands may swell in numbers as more warriors flock to their banner, or existing troops may become more powerful.

After gaining sufficient glory or growing your warband enough to dominate all others through sheer weight of numbers, you will be granted a final test. Succeed, and you will be crowned as the victor of the campaign, your glory affirmed for all time.

CREATING A WARBAND

In a Path to Glory game, you do not select your army in the normal manner. Instead, you create a warband that consists of a mighty champion, battling to earn the favour of the gods, and their followers. The details and progress of each warband need to be recorded on a warband roster, which you can download for free from games-workshop.com.

To create a warband, simply follow these steps and record the results on your warband roster:

1. First, pick a faction for your warband. Each faction has its own set of warband tables that are used to generate the units in the warband and the rewards they can receive for fighting battles. The warband tables included in this battletome let you collect a Tzeentch warband, but other Warhammer Age of Sigmar publications include warband tables to let you collect warbands from other factions.

2. Next, choose your warband's champion by selecting one of the options from your faction's champion table. Give your champion a suitably grand name and write this down on your warband roster.

3. Having picked your champion, the next step is to make follower rolls to generate your starting followers. The champion you chose in step 2 will determine how many follower rolls you have. To make a follower roll, pick a column from one of the followers tables and then roll a dice. If you prefer, instead of rolling a dice, you can pick the result from the followers table (this still uses up the roll).

Sometimes a table will require you to expend two or more rolls, or one roll and a number of Glory Points (see Gaining Glory), in order to use it. Note that the option to expend Glory Points can only be used when you add new followers to your army after a battle (see Rewards of Battle). In either case, in order to generate a follower unit from the table, you must have enough rolls and/or Glory Points to meet the requirements, and you can then either roll once on the table or pick one result from the table of your choice. If you expend Glory Points, you must reduce your Glory Points total by the amount shown on the table.

Followers are organised into units. The followers table tells you how many models the unit has.

Follower units cannot include additional models, but they can otherwise take any options allowed by their warscroll. Record all of the information about your followers on your warband roster.

4. You can use 1 follower roll to allow your champion to start the campaign with a Champion's Reward or to allow 1 of your follower units to start the campaign with a Follower's Reward (see Rewards of Battle).

5. Finally, give your warband a name, one that will inspire respect and dread in your rivals. Your warband is now complete and you can fight your first battle. Good luck!

TO WAR!

Having created a warband, you can now fight battles with it against other warbands taking part in the campaign. You can fight battles as and when you wish, and you can use any of the battleplans available for Warhammer Age of Sigmar. The units you use for a game must be those on your roster.

When you use a Tzeentch warband in a Path to Glory game, you can use the battle traits from pages 69-71, but you cannot use any other Tzeentch allegiance abilities.

Any casualties suffered by a warband are assumed to have been replaced in time for its next battle. If your champion is slain in a battle, it is assumed that they were merely injured; they are back to full strength for your next game, thirsty for vengeance!

GAINING GLORY

All of the players in the campaign are vying for glory. The amount of glory they have received is represented by the Glory Points that the warband has accumulated. As a warband's glory increases, it will also attract additional followers, and a warband's champion may be granted rewards.

Warbands receive Glory Points after a battle is complete. If the warband drew or lost the battle, it receives 1 Glory Point. If it won the battle, it receives D3 Glory Points (re-roll a result of 1 if it won a **major victory**).

Add the Glory Points you scored to the total recorded on your roster. Once you have won 10 Glory Points, you will have a chance to win the campaign (see Eternal Glory).

REWARDS OF BATTLE

After each battle, you can take one of the three following options. Alternatively, roll a D3 to determine which option to take.

D3	Option
1	**Additional Followers:** *More loyal followers flock to your banner.*

You receive 1 follower roll that can be used to select a new unit from a followers table and add it to your warband roster. See step 3 of Creating a Warband for details of how to use the followers table to add a unit to your warband. Once 5 new units

have joined your warband, you will have a chance to win the campaign (see Eternal Glory).

2	**Champion's Reward:** *Your champion's prowess grows.*

Roll on the champion rewards table for your warband and note the result on your warband roster. Your champion can only receive 1 Champion's Reward – if they already have a Champion's Reward, you must take a Follower's Reward instead.

3	**Follower's Reward:** *Your warriors become renowned for their mighty deeds.*

Pick 1 unit of followers and then roll on the followers rewards table for your warband. Note the result on your warband roster. A unit can only receive 1 Follower's Reward. If all of your follower units have a Follower's Reward, you must take Additional Followers instead.

ETERNAL GLORY

There are two ways to win a Path to Glory campaign: by Blood or by Might. To win by Blood,

your warband must first have 10 Glory Points. To win by Might, your warband must have at least 5 additional units of followers. In either case, you must then fight and win one more battle to win the campaign. If the next battle you fight is tied or lost, you do not receive any Glory Points – just keep on fighting battles until you win the campaign… or another player wins first!

You can shorten or lengthen a campaign by lowering or raising the number of Glory Points needed to win by Blood or the number of extra units that must join a warband to win by Might. For example, for a shorter campaign, you could say that a warband only needs 5 Glory Points before the final fight, or for a longer one, you could say that 15 are needed.

TZEENTCH WARBAND TABLES

Use the following tables to determine the champion that leads your warband, the followers that make up the units that fight at their side, and the rewards they receive after battle.

CHAMPION TABLE

Daemon Champion	Follower Rolls
Lord of Change	3 rolls
Fluxmaster, Herald of Tzeentch on Disc	4 rolls
Changecaster, Herald of Tzeentch	5 rolls
Fateskimmer, Herald of Tzeentch on Burning Chariot	5 rolls
Gaunt Summoner of Tzeentch	5 rolls
Arcanite Champion	Follower Rolls
Fatemaster	5 rolls
Magister on Disc of Tzeentch	5 rolls
Tzaangor Shaman	5 rolls

RETINUE FOLLOWERS TABLE

D6	Arcanites	Daemons
1	10 Kairic Acolytes	10 Brimstone Horrors
2	10 Kairic Acolytes	10 Blue Horrors
3	10 Tzaangors	10 Pink Horrors
4	10 Tzaangors	3 Flamers of Tzeentch
5	3 Tzaangor Enlightened	3 Screamers of Tzeentch
6	3 Tzaangor Skyfires	Burning Chariot of Tzeentch

HERO FOLLOWERS TABLE

D6	Arcanites	Daemons
1-2	Tzaangor Shaman	Changecaster, Herald of Tzeentch
3	Magister	Changecaster, Herald of Tzeentch
4	Fatemaster	Fluxmaster, Herald of Tzeentch on Disc
5	Curseling, Eye of Tzeentch	Fluxmaster, Herald of Tzeentch on Disc
6	Ogroid Thaumaturge	Fateskimmer, Herald of Tzeentch on Burning Chariot

ARCANITE HERO FOLLOWERS & RETINUE FOLLOWERS REWARDS TABLE

D3 Reward

1 Nexus of Fate: *These followers manipulate what mortals consider 'destiny' as if it were a puppet.*

At the start of your hero phase, if this unit is on the battlefield, you can roll a dice. If you do so, you can replace one of your Destiny Dice with that roll.

2 Soul Burn: *The slightest contact with these warriors' blades can blight the very fabric of the victim's body.*

If the unmodified hit roll for an attack made with a melee weapon by this unit is 6, that attack inflicts 1 mortal wound on the target in addition to any normal damage.

3 Thieves of All Things Arcane: *Driven by a unquenchable thirst for knowledge, there is no sorcery these followers do not seek to take for their own.*

This unit can attempt to unbind 1 spell in the enemy hero phase. In addition, in the first, third and fifth battle rounds, when this unit attempts to unbind a spell, the spell is automatically unbound (do not roll 2D6).

DAEMON HERO FOLLOWERS & RETINUE FOLLOWERS REWARDS TABLE

D3	Reward
1	**Nexus of Fate:** *These followers manipulate what mortals consider 'destiny' as if it were a puppet.* At the start of your hero phase, if this unit is on the battlefield, you can roll a dice. If you do so, you can replace one of your Destiny Dice with that roll.
2	**Storm of Daemonic Fire:** *So great is the roiling tide of warpfire surrounding these followers that to merely stand in their presence is to risk being set alight.* At the end of the charge phase, roll a dice for each enemy unit within 9" of this unit. On a 6, that unit suffers D3 mortal wounds.
3	**Incorporeal Form:** *These followers can transform into a translucent state when malevolent sorcery draws near.* Each time this unit is affected by a spell or endless spell, you can roll a dice. On a 5+, ignore the effects of that spell or endless spell on this unit.

DAEMON CHAMPION REWARDS TABLE

D3	Reward
1	**Phantasmal Weapons:** *This champion's strikes can pass through armour to cleave the flesh beneath.* Improve the Rend characteristic of this champion's melee weapons by 1.
2	**Warpfire Blade:** *The flames that flicker around this champion's blade can ignite the soul of its victim.* Pick 1 of this champion's melee weapons. If the unmodified hit roll for an attack made with that weapon is 6, that attack inflicts 2 mortal wounds on the target in addition to any normal damage.
3	**Aura of Mutability:** *Even the slightest injury serves as an opportunity for bountiful change when in close proximity to this champion.* Add 1 to wound rolls for attacks made by friendly **Tzeentch Daemon** units that are wholly within 9" of this champion.

ARCANITE CHAMPION REWARDS TABLE

D3	Reward
1	**Spiteful Shield:** *This shield exemplifies Tzeentch's predilection for cruel twists of fate.* If the unmodified save roll for an attack that targets this champion is 6, the attacking unit suffers 2 mortal wounds after all of its attacks have been resolved.
2	**Secret-eater:** *Should this weapon slay one touched by fate, its bearer inherits a measure of their destiny.* Pick 1 of this champion's weapons. If the unmodified hit roll for an attack made with that weapon is 6, you can roll a dice and add it to your Destiny Dice.
3	**Timeslip Pendant:** *Time is a mutable concept to the bearer of this amulet.* Once per battle, at the end of the combat phase, you can say that this champion will enter a timeslip. If you do so, this champion can fight for a second time.

WARSCROLLS

FATE LEGION

As they burst forth from the Impossible Fortress, the manic cackling of the Fate Legion fills their enemies with dread. None but those embraced by change can know what they plan to unleash – only that it will not end well.

ORGANISATION

- 1 Overseer's Fate-twisters warscroll battalion

- 8 warscroll battalions in any combination chosen from the following list:
  - Warpflame Host
  - Multitudinous Host
  - Aether-eater Host
  - Changehost

ABILITIES

'Three times three, the offerings be': *The sacred number of Tzeentch, writ large within the fabric of the Fate Legion, draws one of the many thousands of eyes of their patron – and with it, his favour.*

If your army includes this battalion, you start the battle with 9 Fate Points.

This section includes Disciples of Tzeentch warscrolls, warscroll battalions and endless spell warscrolls. Updated January 2020; the warscrolls printed here take precedence over any warscrolls with an earlier publication date or no publication date.

*D*aellan the Teller spasmed in his sleep, haunted by the dream once more. Hideous forms writhed and burned in the catacombs under the city. Avian heads on wattled necks cried out in evil glee, creatures of sentient fire lit the dank caves, flame-spewing monsters burned the moss-damp walls dry in their haste to incinerate living things. The gangling Horrors that formed the vast majority of the daemon host crawled up the walls of the caves, cartwheeling vertically upwards and bounding amongst the stalactites. Seen together, they were like a spreading pool of multicoloured flame, drawn up the walls in defiance of gravity as their feathered masters took flight. The vision was clearer than ever before. Daellan awoke with a jolt, his blankets damp with sweat. This time he was certain it was real.

His heart fluttering like a trapped bird, Daellan rushed over to the thin triangular window of his garret and threw open the shutters. To his profound relief, the Watchberg Blackhelms were already on the march, a phalanx of gleaming Stormcast Eternals at their fore.

Then the young man noticed the armed column was heading toward the north gate. The flapping bird of panic within his ribcage returned, frantic, as he watched them leave. From his high vantage point, he could see the gates being slammed shut and barred with heavy oaken beams by men wearing grotesque golden masks.

Only then did he see the multicoloured smoke curling from the cobblestones and the daemons crawling from the earth. Watchberg would burn.

WARSCROLL BATTALION
WARPFLAME HOST

ORGANISATION

- 1 unit of Exalted Flamers of Tzeentch

- 3-8 units in any combination chosen from the following list:
  - Exalted Flamers of Tzeentch
  - Flamers of Tzeentch
  - Burning Chariots of Tzeentch

ABILITIES

Storm of Daemonic Fire: *So great is the roiling tide of warpfire surrounding a Warpflame Host that to merely stand in the daemons' presence is to risk being set alight. Those who burn swiftly can be reckoned as the lucky ones.*

At the end of the charge phase, roll a dice for each enemy unit within 9" of any friendly units from this battalion. On a 6, that enemy unit suffers D3 mortal wounds.

WARSCROLL BATTALION
MULTITUDINOUS HOST

ORGANISATION

- 1 Changecaster, Herald of Tzeentch

- 8 units of Horrors of Tzeentch

ABILITIES

Horrors Without Number: *So concentrated is the change-magic that swirls about a Multitudinous Host that ever more Horrors pop into existence around them, their numbers swelling at an alarming rate.*

At the start of your hero phase, you can return D3 slain **HORRORS OF TZEENTCH** models to each friendly **HORRORS OF TZEENTCH** unit from this battalion (roll separately for each unit).

WARSCROLL BATTALION
AETHER-EATER HOST

ORGANISATION

- 1 Fateskimmer, Herald of Tzeentch on Burning Chariot

- 3-8 units in any combination chosen from the following list:
  - The Blue Scribes
  - Fateskimmer, Herald of Tzeentch on Burning Chariot
  - Fluxmaster, Herald of Tzeentch on Disc
  - Screamers of Tzeentch

ABILITIES

Feed on Magic: *Though all daemons are formed of raw magic, those in an Aether-eater Host can drain the sorcerous energies unleashed by their foes to revitalise their physical forms.*

If a friendly unit from this battalion successfully unbinds a spell in the enemy hero phase, you can immediately heal D3 wounds allocated to that unit. In addition, 1 friendly **SCREAMERS OF TZEENTCH** unit from this battalion can attempt to unbind 1 spell in the enemy hero phase.

WARSCROLL BATTALION
CHANGEHOST

ORGANISATION

- 1 Lord of Change

- 8 units in any combination chosen from the following list:
  - **Horror Heroes**
  - Exalted Flamers of Tzeentch
  - Horrors of Tzeentch
  - Flamers of Tzeentch
  - Screamers of Tzeentch
  - Burning Chariots of Tzeentch

ABILITIES

Deceive and Dismay: *Nothing is ever quite as it seems when fighting against the forces of Tzeentch, and this is doubly true when facing a Changehost. In the blink of an eye, the daemons will shimmer and disappear from sight, only to be reappear where their Lord of Change master requires them.*

At the start of your hero phase, if the **Lord of Change** from this battalion is your general and is on the battlefield, you can pick 2 other friendly units from this battalion and remove them from the battlefield. If you do so, set up those units again anywhere on the battlefield more than 9" from any enemy units. The units you set up cannot move in the following movement phase.

WARSCROLL BATTALION
OVERSEER'S FATE-TWISTERS

ORGANISATION

- 1 Lord of Change

- 8 units in any combination chosen from the following list:
  - **Horror Heroes**
  - Exalted Flamers of Tzeentch
  - Burning Chariots of Tzeentch

ABILITIES

The Will of Tzeentch: *The Lords of Change known as the Overseers, together with their most accomplished lieutenants, bear the favour of the Great Conspirator – the better to enact his will in all things. To them, the skeins of fate are as the strings of a lyre to be plucked at a whim.*

At the start of your hero phase, if 1 or more friendly units from this battalion are on the battlefield, you can roll a dice and add it to your Destiny Dice. In addition, at the start of your hero phase, if the **Lord of Change** from this battalion is on the battlefield, you can re-roll one of your Destiny Dice.

WARSCROLL BATTALION
OMNISCIENT ORACLES

ORGANISATION

- Kairos Fateweaver

- 3 Lords of Change

ABILITIES

Knowledge of the Past, Present and Future: *Kairos Fateweaver sees both the past and the future, and in sealing a soul-binding pact with the Lords of Change known as the Allscryers, Kairos has ensured the deeds of the moment are made clear to him as well.*

You can re-roll hit, wound and save rolls of 1 for friendly units from this battalion.

WARSCROLL BATTALION
ARCANITE CULT

When the preparations have been made, the dark bargains struck and the time deemed right, an Arcanite Cult will finally reveal itself – and, in doing so, go to war.

ORGANISATION

- 1 Arcanite Cabal warscroll battalion

- 8 warscroll battalions in any combination chosen from the following list:
  - Alter-kin Coven
  - Skyshoal Coven
  - Tzaangor Coven
  - Witchfyre Coven

ABILITIES

Destiny Preordained: *When the Arcanites attack in their full might, it is done at a crux point of destiny – perhaps a sorcerous equinox or daemon convergence – to better fulfil a purpose that the Change God has long foreseen.*

If your army includes this battalion, instead of rolling 9 dice for the Masters of Destiny battle trait (pg 69), you can choose the values of 6 of the Destiny Dice and then roll the remaining 3 dice as normal.

*L*arian Coinbiter grinned behind the rough, itchy cloth of his bandana as the winding caravans of the Serpentine City finally came to a halt, ready for the victory celebration. They had overcome the flame-spewing daemons that had harried them from the crevasses and fissures on either side of the trade route. Larian had helped defeat them himself; he was no mean shot with a crossbow. But little did the nomad masters realise that it was he who had summoned them in the first place.

Skylighter rockets traded from Greywater Fastness burst in patterns high overhead, lighting the clouds as the revellers donned their masks and emerged from the caravans to dance in the red dust of the Odrenn plain. Jugs of alchemical liquor were passed around, swarf-pipes were chugged and plates of roasted hawk dished out. Then the joyous singing that reached the night skies took on a different timbre, as counter-rhythms and bleating calls in the Tzaangor tongue came echoing from the canyon's giant boulders.

A piercing cry ripped the air, and the Cult of the Writhing Serpent took their blades to caravan guards drowsy from poison-spiked wine. Larian called a bolt of fire into being and hurled it at a canvas caravan roof, his fellow cultists following suit. The Tzaangors closed in at the signal. Dozens of caravans burned, together forming a snake of fire several leagues in length. Larian screamed to the skies in triumph.

High above, the flames of the skylighter rockets twisted into the visage of a tentacle-horned god – and smiled.

WARSCROLL BATTALION
ARCANITE CABAL

ORGANISATION

- 3-9 models in any combination chosen from the following list:
  - Fatemaster
  - **Magister**
  - Tzaangor Shaman

ABILITIES

Master of the Cult: *The cult's leader wears Tzeentch's favour like a mantle. To him, the future is a many-branched pathway to be walked at leisure.*

After armies have been set up but before the first battle round begins, pick 1 friendly model from this battalion. For the rest of the battle, each time you spend a Destiny Dice to replace a dice roll for that model, roll a dice. On a 2+, you can replace one of your remaining Destiny Dice with that roll.

WARSCROLL BATTALION
ALTER-KIN COVEN

ORGANISATION

- 1 unit of Kairic Acolytes

- 1 unit of Tzaangors

- 1 unit of Tzaangor Skyfires

ABILITIES

Boon of Mutation: *Enemies of an Alter-kin Coven are under the constant threat of mutation, the unluckiest of them ending up transmogrified into a Tzaangor.*

At the end of the charge phase, roll a dice for each enemy unit within 3" of a friendly unit from this battalion. On a 6, that unit suffers D3 mortal wounds. If any models are slain by this ability, before removing the first slain model, you can add 1 **Tzaangor** model to an existing **Tzaangor** unit in your army. If you do so, set up that **Tzaangor** model within 1" of a friendly **Tzaangor** unit that is within 9" of the slain model. The model can only be set up within 3" of an enemy unit if the friendly **Tzaangor** unit was within 3" of that enemy unit before any models were added.

WARSCROLL BATTALION
WITCHFYRE COVEN

ORGANISATION

- 3 units of Kairic Acolytes

- 1 unit of Tzaangor Enlightened

ABILITIES

Mastery of Wyrdflame: *The Kairic Acolytes that form a Witchfyre Coven are highly skilled at conjuring the flames of change. They are able to assail their foes with a relentless bombardment of eldritch fire.*

Once per turn, in your hero phase, you can pick 1 friendly **Kairic Acolyte** unit from this battalion. That unit can shoot.

WARSCROLL BATTALION
SKYSHOAL COVEN

ORGANISATION

- 2 units of Tzaangor Enlightened on Discs of Tzeentch

- 2 units of Tzaangor Skyfires

ABILITIES

Diving from the Skies: *The Tzaangor Enlightened and Skyfires of the Skyshoal Covens have learnt to utilise the blade-like protrusions of their daemonic mounts to lethal effect.*

After a friendly unit from this battalion has made a normal move, you can pick 1 enemy unit that has any models passed across by any models from that friendly unit and roll a dice. On a 2+, that enemy unit suffers D3 mortal wounds.

WARSCROLL BATTALION
TZAANGOR COVEN

ORGANISATION

- 2 units of Tzaangors

- 2 units of Tzaangor Enlightened

- 2 units of Tzaangor Skyfires

ABILITIES

Pride of the Gor-kin: *Widely considered to be the greatest of Tzeentch's mortal followers, these avian beastmen fight with an unrivalled ferocity borne from their limitless confidence.*

At the start of your hero phase, you can pick 1 friendly unit from this battalion that is within 3" of an enemy unit. That unit can shoot or fight.

LORD OF CHANGE

The greatest of Tzeentch's daemons, the Lords of Change shimmer with raw magic. With a flick of their claw, they can hurl foes into the nightmarish Realm of Chaos, blast enemies with wyrdfire or steal opponents' spells for their own use.

MOVE 14

SAVE 4+

WOUNDS 10

BRAVERY

98

MISSILE WEAPONS	Range	Attacks	To Hit	To Wound	Rend	Damage
Rod of Sorcery	18"	2D6	3+	3+	-1	1
MELEE WEAPONS	Range	Attacks	To Hit	To Wound	Rend	Damage
Staff of Tzeentch	3"	4	3+	☀	-	2
Baleful Sword	1"	2	4+	2+	-2	3
Curved Beak and Wicked Talons	1"	4	4+	3+	-1	2

DAMAGE TABLE			
Wounds Suffered	Move	Staff of Tzeentch	Infernal Gateway
0-3	12"	1+	3+
4-6	10"	2+	4+
7-9	9"	3+	4+
10-12	8"	4+	4+
13+	7"	5+	5+

DESCRIPTION

A Lord of Change is a single model armed with one of the following weapon options: Staff of Tzeentch and Baleful Sword; Staff of Tzeentch and Rod of Sorcery; or Staff of Tzeentch and Curved Beak and Wicked Talons.

FLY: This model can fly.

ABILITIES

Mastery of Magic: *To master the arcane is to embody the grand design of the Changer of the Ways.*

When this model makes a casting, unbinding or dispelling roll, you can change the lowest D6 to match the highest D6.

Spell-eater: *Tzeentch's daemons revel in the Arcanum Optimar, summoning and dispelling even the most predatory spells at will.*

Once per turn, in your hero phase, you can pick 1 endless spell within 18" of this model. That endless spell is dispelled.

Spell-thief: *Should a rival sorcerer conjure a spell that intrigues the Lord of Change, the greater daemon will acquire the incantation for its own use.*

If this model successfully unbinds an enemy spell with an unbinding roll of 9+, this model can attempt to cast that spell, if it is possible for it to do so, for the rest of the battle.

MAGIC

This model is a **WIZARD**. It can attempt to cast 2 spells in your hero phase and attempt to unbind 2 spells in the enemy hero phase. It knows the Arcane Bolt, Mystic Shield and Infernal Gateway spells.

Infernal Gateway: *The Lord of Change opens a portal to the Realm of Chaos, pulling enemies to their doom.*

Infernal Gateway has a casting value of 7. If successfully cast, pick 1 enemy unit within 18" of the caster that is visible to them and roll 9 dice. That unit suffers 1 mortal wound for each roll that is equal to or greater than the Infernal Gateway value shown on the caster's damage table.

COMMAND ABILITY

Beacon of Sorcery: *Spreading its arms wide, the Lord of Change saturates the area with raw magic.*

You can use this command ability at the start of your hero phase. If you do so, pick 1 friendly model with this command ability. Until your next hero phase, you can add 1 to casting and unbinding rolls for friendly **TZEENTCH DAEMON WIZARDS** while they are wholly within 18" of that model.

KEYWORDS	CHAOS, DAEMON, TZEENTCH, MONSTER, HERO, WIZARD, LORD OF CHANGE

KAIROS FATEWEAVER

99

Kairos Fateweaver can see the past and the future, and he uses this ability to twist destiny to suit his own malevolent purposes. The twin-headed terror is a master of magic known as the Oracle of Tzeentch – wherever he goes, change is sure to follow.

MELEE WEAPONS	Range	Attacks	To Hit	To Wound	Rend	Damage
Staff of Tomorrow	3"	3	3+	☀	-1	2
Beaks and Claws	1"	5	4+	3+	-1	2

DAMAGE TABLE			
Wounds Suffered	Move	Staff of Tomorrow	Gift of Change
0-3	12"	1+	6
4-6	10"	2+	D6
7-9	9"	3+	3
10-12	8"	4+	D3
13+	7"	5+	1

DESCRIPTION

Kairos Fateweaver is a named character that is a single model. He is armed with the Staff of Tomorrow and his Beaks and Claws.

FLY: This model can fly.

ABILITIES

Mastery of Magic: *To master the arcane is to embody the grand design of the Changer of the Ways.*

When this model makes a casting, unbinding or dispelling roll, you can change the lowest D6 to match the highest D6.

Spell-eater: *Tzeentch's daemons revel in the Arcanum Optimar, summoning and dispelling even the most predatory spells at will.*

Once per turn, in your hero phase, you can pick 1 endless spell within 18" of this model. That endless spell is dispelled.

Oracle of Eternity: *The oracle uses his insight to guide reality into fulfilling his own prophecies. A single twist in fate can mean utter devastation to any who cross Kairos.*

Once per battle, in either player's turn, if this model is on the battlefield, you can replace a single dice from one of the following dice rolls with a result of your choice.

- Casting rolls
- Unbinding rolls
- Dispelling rolls
- Run rolls
- Charge rolls
- Hit rolls
- Wound rolls
- Save rolls
- Any roll that determines the Damage characteristic of a missile or melee weapon
- Battleshock tests

Note that this ability only allows you to replace a single dice roll. For 2D6 rolls (such as casting rolls or charge rolls), you can only replace 1 of the dice. In addition, any rolls that have been replaced count as unmodified rolls and cannot be re-rolled or modified further.

MAGIC

Kairos Fateweaver is a **WIZARD**. He can attempt to cast 3 spells in your hero phase and attempt to unbind 3 spells in the enemy hero phase. He knows the Arcane Bolt, Mystic Shield and Gift of Change spells.

In addition, while friendly **WIZARDS** are wholly within 18" of him, Kairos Fateweaver knows any spells on those **WIZARDS'** warscrolls that are possible for him to cast.

Gift of Change: *As Kairos traces a burning sigil in the air, he gifts his foes the boon of mutating flesh.*

Gift of Change has a casting value of 8. If successfully cast, pick 1 enemy unit within 18" of the caster and visible to them. That unit suffers a number of mortal wounds equal to the Gift of Change value shown on the caster's damage table. If any models were slain by this spell, before removing the first slain model, you can add a **TZEENTCH CHAOS SPAWN** to your army and set it up within 3" of the slain model's unit.

KEYWORDS	CHAOS, DAEMON, TZEENTCH, MONSTER, HERO, WIZARD, LORD OF CHANGE, KAIROS FATEWEAVER

GAUNT SUMMONER OF TZEENTCH

MOVE	5"
WOUNDS	5
SAVE	6+
BRAVERY	8

There are but nine Gaunt Summoners, a powerful order of sorcerers dedicated to Tzeentch. Gazing into infinity with a myriad glistening eyes, a Gaunt Summoner calls forth daemons or summons sheets of infernal flames to engulf the foe.

MISSILE WEAPONS	Range	Attacks	To Hit	To Wound	Rend	Damage
Changestaff	18"	1	3+	4+	-	D3
MELEE WEAPONS	Range	Attacks	To Hit	To Wound	Rend	Damage
Warptongue Blade	1"	1	3+	4+	-	1

DESCRIPTION

A Gaunt Summoner of Tzeentch is a single model armed with a Changestaff and Warptongue Blade.

ABILITIES

Warptongue Blade: *Those cut by a warptongue blade soon find their bodies wracked with sickening and uncontrollable mutations.*

If the unmodified wound roll for an attack made with a Warptongue Blade is 6, that attack inflicts D6 mortal wounds on the target and the attack sequence ends (do not make a save roll).

Book of Profane Secrets: *Whispering fell incantations, a Gaunt Summoner can temporarily divert the path of a Realmgate, allowing malefic Chaos entities to manifest on the battlefield.*

Once per battle, at the start of your hero phase, you can say that this model will use its Book of Profane Secrets. If you do so, you can summon 1 unit from the list below to the battlefield and add it to your army, but the number of spells that this model can attempt to cast in that phase is reduced by 1. The summoned unit must be set up wholly within 9" of this model and more than 9" from any enemy units.

Choose 1 unit from the following list:

- 10 Pink Horrors
- 10 Bloodletters
- 10 Plaguebearers
- 10 Daemonettes
- 6 Furies

MAGIC

This model is a **WIZARD**. It can attempt to cast 2 spells in your hero phase and attempt to unbind 2 spells in the enemy hero phase. It knows the Arcane Bolt, Mystic Shield and Infernal Flames spells.

Infernal Flames: *The Gaunt Summoner conjures a rolling wave of scorching wyrdfire that engulfs enemy formations.*

Infernal Flames has a casting value of 7. If successfully cast, pick 1 enemy unit within 12" of the caster that is visible to them, and roll 1 dice for each model in that unit. For each 5+, that unit suffers 1 mortal wound. If that unit is an enemy **MONSTER** or **WAR MACHINE**, roll 3 dice for each model instead.

KEYWORDS	CHAOS, DAEMON, MORTAL, TZEENTCH, ARCANITE, SLAVES TO DARKNESS, EVERCHOSEN, HERO, WIZARD, GAUNT SUMMONER

FATESKIMMER
HERALD OF TZEENTCH ON BURNING CHARIOT

MOVE 16"
WOUNDS 8
SAVE 5+
BRAVERY 10

101

Trailing flames and maniacal laughter, a Fateskimmer streaks across the skies. While the Herald conjures firestorms to engulf the foe, the living chariot it rides seeks to sear all those in its path, the Screamers at its fore biting their prey as they speed by.

MISSILE WEAPONS	Range	Attacks	To Hit	To Wound	Rend	Damage
Magical Flames	18"	3	4+	4+	-1	1
MELEE WEAPONS	**Range**	**Attacks**	**To Hit**	**To Wound**	**Rend**	**Damage**
Staff of Change	2"	1	4+	3+	-1	D3
Ritual Dagger	1"	2	4+	4+	-	1
Lamprey Bite	1"	6	4+	3+	-	1

DESCRIPTION

A Fateskimmer, Herald of Tzeentch on Burning Chariot, is a single model armed with Magical Flames, Staff of Change and Ritual Dagger.

MOUNT: This model's Screamers of Tzeentch attack with their Lamprey Bites.

FLY: This model can fly.

ABILITIES

Arcane Tome: *This arcane tome holds scriptures of ancient incantation that allows a brief mastery of the Herald's chosen spell lores.*

Once per battle, when this model attempts to cast or unbind a spell, you can roll 3D6, remove 1 dice of your choice, and then use the remaining 2D6 to determine the casting or unbinding roll.

Sky-sharks: *Screamers that manage to sink their teeth into a larger creature will not let go easily, eventually tearing off huge chunks of bloodied flesh.*

If the target is an enemy **MONSTER**, change the Damage characteristic of this model's Lamprey Bite to D3.

Wake of Fire: *Enemies unfortunate enough to be passed by a Burning Chariot are consumed by waves of unnatural fire.*

After this model has made a normal move, you can pick 1 enemy unit that has any models passed across by this model and roll a dice. On a 2+, that unit suffers D3 mortal wounds.

MAGIC

This model is a **WIZARD**. It can attempt to cast 1 spell in your hero phase and attempt to unbind 1 spell in the enemy hero phase. It knows the Arcane Bolt, Mystic Shield and Tzeentch's Firestorm spells.

Tzeentch's Firestorm: *Searing balls of scarlet flame whip around the caster before spiralling outwards to engulf nearby enemies.*

Tzeentch's Firestorm has a casting value of 8. If successfully cast, roll a dice for each enemy unit within 9" of the caster and visible to them. On a 3+, that unit suffers D3 mortal wounds.

KEYWORDS	CHAOS, DAEMON, HORROR, TZEENTCH, HERO, WIZARD, FATESKIMMER

FLUXMASTER
HERALD OF TZEENTCH ON DISC

MOVE	16"
WOUNDS	6
SAVE	5+
BRAVERY	10

102

There is nowhere on the battlefield safe from a Herald riding a Disc of Tzeentch. Bolting through the air, the Fluxmaster conjures blue flames to hurl at the foe before darting in to deliver a swift blow from a mutative Staff of Change.

MISSILE WEAPONS	Range	Attacks	To Hit	To Wound	Rend	Damage
Magical Flames	18"	3	4+	4+	-1	1
MELEE WEAPONS	Range	Attacks	To Hit	To Wound	Rend	Damage
Staff of Change	2"	1	4+	3+	-1	D3
Ritual Dagger	1"	2	4+	4+	-	1
Teeth and Horns	1"	D3	4+	3+	-1	D3

DESCRIPTION

A Fluxmaster, Herald of Tzeentch on Disc, is a single model armed with Magical Flames and one of the following weapon options: Staff of Change and Arcane Tome; or Ritual Dagger and Arcane Tome.

MOUNT: This model's Disc of Tzeentch attacks with its Teeth and Horns.

FLY: This model can fly.

ABILITIES

Arcane Tome: *This arcane tome holds scriptures of ancient incantation that allows a brief mastery of the herald's chosen spell lores.*

Once per battle, when this model attempts to cast or unbind a spell, you can roll 3D6, remove 1 dice of your choice, and then use the remaining 2D6 to determine the casting or unbinding roll.

MAGIC

This model is a **WIZARD**. It can attempt to cast 1 spell in your hero phase and attempt to unbind 1 spell in the enemy hero phase. It knows the Arcane Bolt, Mystic Shield and Blue Fire of Tzeentch spells.

Blue Fire of Tzeentch: *A tide of iridescent mutating flame surges forth from the Fluxmaster as it cackles from its swooping Disc.*

Blue Fire of Tzeentch has a casting value of 5. If successfully cast, pick 1 enemy unit within 18" of the caster and visible to them, and roll 9 dice. For each 6, that unit suffers 1 mortal wound.

KEYWORDS	CHAOS, DAEMON, HORROR, TZEENTCH, HERO, WIZARD, FLUXMASTER

THE CHANGELING

A master of illusionary disguise, the Changeling hides amongst its quarry, sowing confusion amongst their ranks. Upon throwing aside its fleshly masquerade, the Changeling uses sorcery and its Trickster's Staff to openly blast its foes.

MOVE 5"
WOUNDS 5
SAVE 5+
BRAVERY 10

MELEE WEAPONS	Range	Attacks	To Hit	To Wound	Rend	Damage
The Trickster's Staff	2"	3	3+	3+	-1	D3

DESCRIPTION

The Changeling is a single model armed with the Trickster's Staff.

ABILITIES

Puckish Misdirection: *The Changeling can manipulate the most stalwart of warriors while appearing as a trusted advisor or comrade.*

In the enemy hero phase, you can pick 1 enemy unit within 9" of this model. If you do so, until your next hero phase, subtract 1 from hit rolls for attacks made by that unit and half the Move characteristic of that unit (rounding up).

Arch-deceiver: *None can detect the veil of the Changeling. Assuming the form of comrade and ally, it reveals itself only when its plans have been made a reality.*

At the start of the first battle round, after armies have been set up but before the first turn begins, you can remove this model from the battlefield. If you do so, at the end of your first movement phase, you must set this model up again anywhere within your opponent's territory more than 3" from any enemy units.

MAGIC

This model is a **WIZARD**. It can attempt to cast 2 spells in your hero phase and attempt to unbind 2 spells in the enemy hero phase. It knows the Arcane Bolt and Mystic Shield spells.

In addition, while this model is within 9" of an enemy **WIZARD**, it knows any spells on that **WIZARD**'s warscroll that are possible for this model to cast.

KEYWORDS	CHAOS, DAEMON, HORROR, TZEENTCH, HERO, WIZARD, THE CHANGELING

CHANGECASTER
HERALD OF TZEENTCH

Wielding the pink changefire of its patron, a Herald of Tzeentch is a luminescent servant of the Changer of the Ways. Any that attempt to thwart its anarchic cause will soon feel the wrath of living flames or the mutating blows of its Staff of Change.

MOVE 5"
WOUNDS 5
SAVE 5+
BRAVERY 10

MISSILE WEAPONS	Range	Attacks	To Hit	To Wound	Rend	Damage
Magical Flames	18"	3	4+	4+	-1	1
MELEE WEAPONS	**Range**	**Attacks**	**To Hit**	**To Wound**	**Rend**	**Damage**
Staff of Change	2"	1	4+	3+	-1	D3
Ritual Dagger	1"	2	4+	4+	-	1

DESCRIPTION

A Changecaster, Herald of Tzeentch, is a single model armed with Magical Flames and one of the following weapon options: Staff of Change and Arcane Tome; or Ritual Dagger and Arcane Tome.

ABILITIES

Fortune and Fate: *The sacred number nine blesses any follower practising the arcane.*

If this model successfully casts a spell with a casting roll of 9+, this model can attempt to cast 1 extra spell in that phase.

Arcane Tome: *This arcane tome holds scriptures of ancient incantation that allows a brief mastery of the Herald's chosen spell lores.*

Once per battle, when this model attempts to cast or unbind a spell, you can roll 3D6, remove 1 dice of your choice, and then use the remaining 2D6 to determine the casting or unbinding roll.

MAGIC

This model is a **WIZARD**. It can attempt to cast 1 spell in your hero phase and attempt to unbind 1 spell in the enemy hero phase. It knows the Arcane Bolt, Mystic Shield and Pink Fire of Tzeentch spells.

Pink Fire of Tzeentch: *The Changecaster conjures a tide of writhing warpflame that engulfs the foe.*

Pink Fire of Tzeentch has a casting value of 9. If successfully cast, pick 1 enemy unit within 18" of the caster and visible to them. That unit suffers D6 mortal wounds.

KEYWORDS	CHAOS, DAEMON, HORROR, TZEENTCH, HERO, WIZARD, CHANGECASTER

104

THE BLUE SCRIBES

Tzeentch created two daemons, P'tarix and Xirat'p, for the sole purpose of learning every spell in existence. The Blue Scribes, as they are known, ride their Disc of Tzeentch through the realms seeking every fragment of arcana.

MELEE WEAPONS	Range	Attacks	To Hit	To Wound	Rend	Damage
Sharpened Quills	1"	2	5+	5+	-	1
Teeth and Horns	1"	D3	4+	3+	-1	D3

DESCRIPTION

The Blue Scribes is a single model armed with Sharpened Quills.

MOUNT: This model's Disc of Tzeentch attacks with its Teeth and Horns.

FLY: This model can fly.

ABILITIES

Frantic Scribbling: *The Blue Scribes seek any unknown incantations that might be used against them.*

Each time a **WIZARD** wholly within 18" of this model successfully casts a spell that is not unbound and that is possible for this model to cast, you can roll a dice. On a 4+, this model knows that spell for the rest of the battle.

Scrolls of Sorcery: *The unlimited arcane knowledge held on these scrolls can conjure sorceries of perfect structure.*

Once in each of your hero phases, when this model attempts to cast a spell, instead of making a casting roll, you can say that it will read from its scrolls of sorcery. If you do so, roll a dice. On a 2+, that spell is automatically cast and cannot be unbound.

MAGIC

This model is a **WIZARD**. It can attempt to cast 1 spell in your hero phase and attempt to unbind 1 spell in the enemy hero phase. It knows the Arcane Bolt, Mystic Shield and Boon of Tzeentch spells.

Boon of Tzeentch: *The Blue Scribes reach forth, tapping into an unseen hoard of arcane power.*

Boon of Tzeentch has a casting value of 4. If successfully cast, you can re-roll casting rolls for friendly **TZEENTCH WIZARDS** wholly within 18" of the caster for the rest of that phase.

KEYWORDS	CHAOS, DAEMON, HORROR, TZEENTCH, HERO, WIZARD, THE BLUE SCRIBES

SCREAMERS OF TZEENTCH

Speeding blurs that leave shimmering trails of change-magic in the air, Screamers streak across the skies with a wailing cry. They slash any foes they pass with razor-sharp horns and fins before darting down to savage their chosen quarry.

MELEE WEAPONS	Range	Attacks	To Hit	To Wound	Rend	Damage
Lamprey Bite	1"	3	4+	3+	-	1

DESCRIPTION

A unit of Screamers of Tzeentch has any number of models, each attacking with a Lamprey Bite.

FLY: This unit can fly.

ABILITIES

Sky-sharks: *Screamers that manage to sink their teeth into a larger creature will not let go easily, eventually tearing off huge chunks of bloodied flesh.*

If the target is an enemy **MONSTER**, change the Damage characteristic of this unit's Lamprey Bite to D3.

Slashing Fins: *The pack mentality of Screamers makes them an especially effective unit on the battlefield. They swoop in formation and slash at their foes, performing fly-by attacks and effortless manoeuvres.*

After this unit has made a normal move, pick 1 enemy unit and roll 1 dice for each model in this unit that passed across any models from that unit. For each 5+, that unit suffers 1 mortal wound. If that enemy unit is a **WIZARD**, for each 5+, inflict D3 mortal wounds instead of 1.

KEYWORDS	CHAOS, DAEMON, TZEENTCH, SCREAMERS

BURNING CHARIOTS OF TZEENTCH

105

Drawn through the skies by a pair of Screamers, a Burning Chariot rides upon a wave of multicoloured flames that scorches all in its wake, while the Exalted Flamer that writhes and twists upon its back breathes out sheets of unnatural, billowing fire.

MOVE 14"
WOUNDS 6
SAVE 5+
BRAVERY 10

MISSILE WEAPONS	Range	Attacks	To Hit	To Wound	Rend	Damage
Billowing Warpflame	18"	6	4+	3+	-1	D3
MELEE WEAPONS	**Range**	**Attacks**	**To Hit**	**To Wound**	**Rend**	**Damage**
Flaming Maw	2"	4	5+	3+	-	1
Blue Horrors' Jabs	1"	3	5+	5+	-	1
Lamprey Bite	1"	6	4+	3+	-	1

DESCRIPTION

A unit of Burning Chariots of Tzeentch has any number of models, each armed with Billowing Warpflame, Flaming Maws and Blue Horror's Jabs.

MOUNT: This unit's Screamers of Tzeentch attack with their Lamprey Bites.

FLY: This unit can fly.

ABILITIES

Capricious Warpflame: *These unnatural fires continue to burn long after they meet their target, clawing at the nearest foe as a Fury would its prey.*

Add 1 to hit rolls for attacks made by this unit if the target unit has 10 or more models. Add 2 to hit rolls instead of 1 if the target unit has 20 or more models.

Sky-sharks: *Screamers that manage to sink their teeth into a larger creature will not let go easily, eventually tearing off huge chunks of bloodied flesh.*

If the target is an enemy **Monster**, change the Damage characteristic of this unit's Lamprey Bite to D3.

Touched by Fire: *When forced to meet an enemy in hand-to-hand combat, Flamers rely on their blazing forms to repel their foe.*

Roll a dice each time you allocate a wound or mortal wound to this unit that was inflicted by a melee weapon. On a 5+, the attacking unit suffers 1 mortal wound.

Wake of Fire: *Enemies unfortunate enough to be passed by a Burning Chariot are flooded with waves of unnatural fire.*

After this unit has made a normal move, you can pick 1 enemy unit that has any models passed across by any models from this unit and roll a dice. On a 2+, that enemy unit suffers D3 mortal wounds.

KEYWORDS	CHAOS, DAEMON, FLAMER, EXALTED FLAMERS, HORROR, TZEENTCH, BURNING CHARIOTS

EXALTED FLAMERS OF TZEENTCH

MOVE 9"
WOUNDS 4
SAVE 5+
BRAVERY 10

106

An Exalted Flamer can project gouts of multicoloured flame, turning entire enemy units into piles of blackened bones. The shifting warpflames seem to have a mind of their own, forming hideous faces and ominous sigils with their tongues of fire.

MISSILE WEAPONS	Range	Attacks	To Hit	To Wound	Rend	Damage
Billowing Warpflame	18"	6	4+	3+	-1	D3
MELEE WEAPONS	Range	Attacks	To Hit	To Wound	Rend	Damage
Flaming Maw	2"	4	5+	3+	-	1

DESCRIPTION

A unit of Exalted Flamers of Tzeentch has any number of models, each armed with Billowing Warpflame and Flaming Maws.

FLY: This unit can fly.

ABILITIES

Capricious Warpflame: *These unnatural fires continue to burn long after they meet their target, clawing at the nearest foe as a Fury would its prey.*

Add 1 to hit rolls for attacks made by this unit if the target unit has 10 or more models. Add 2 to hit rolls instead of 1 if the target unit has 20 or more models.

Touched by Fire: *When forced to meet an enemy in hand-to-hand combat, Flamers rely on their blazing forms to repel their foe.*

Roll a dice each time you allocate a wound or mortal wound to this unit that was inflicted by a melee weapon. On a 5+, the attacking unit suffers 1 mortal wound.

KEYWORDS	CHAOS, DAEMON, FLAMER, TZEENTCH, EXALTED FLAMERS

FLAMERS OF TZEENTCH

MOVE 9"
WOUNDS 2
SAVE 5+
BRAVERY 10

Bounding in a disturbing fashion, Flamers of Tzeentch spring towards the foe spouting the warpfires of Chaos. Yet the Changer of the Ways is fickle, and fires that have burnt out may once more leap to life, guiding even more flames to the target.

MISSILE WEAPONS	Range	Attacks	To Hit	To Wound	Rend	Damage
Warpflame	18"	3	4+	3+	-	D3
MELEE WEAPONS	Range	Attacks	To Hit	To Wound	Rend	Damage
Flaming Maw	1"	2	5+	3+	-	1

DESCRIPTION

A unit of Flamers of Tzeentch has any number of models, each armed with Warpflame and Flaming Maws.

PYROCASTER: 1 model in this unit can be a Pyrocaster. Add 1 to the Attacks characteristic of that model's missile weapon.

FLY: This unit can fly.

ABILITIES

Capricious Warpflame: *These unnatural fires continue to burn long after they meet their target, clawing at the nearest foe as a Fury would its prey.*

Add 1 to hit rolls for attacks made by this unit if the target unit has 10 or more models. Add 2 to hit rolls instead of 1 if the target unit has 20 or more models.

Touched by Fire: *When forced to meet an enemy in hand-to-hand combat, Flamers rely on their blazing forms to repel their foe.*

Roll a dice each time you allocate a wound or mortal wound to this unit that was inflicted by a melee weapon. On a 5+, the attacking unit suffers 1 mortal wound.

Guided by Billowing Flames: *If their Exalted kin are nearby, Flamers can follow their blazing trails to increase the intensity of their fires.*

Add 1 to hit rolls for attacks made with this unit's Warpflame while it is wholly within 9" of any friendly **EXALTED FLAMERS**.

KEYWORDS	CHAOS, DAEMON, FLAMER, TZEENTCH, FLAMERS OF TZEENTCH

HORRORS OF TZEENTCH

Gibbering with lunatic energy, the luminescent Pink Horrors whirl and flail, generating raw magic that can manifest as blasts of unnatural fire that scour the enemy. Should they be slain, Horrors split in twain to form two lesser incarnations.

MISSILE WEAPONS	Range	Attacks	To Hit	To Wound	Rend	Damage
Magical Flames	12"	☀	5+	4+	-	1
MELEE WEAPONS	Range	Attacks	To Hit	To Wound	Rend	Damage
Taloned Hands	1"	☀	5+	4+	-	1

HORROR TABLE		
Horror Colour	Magical Flames	Taloned Hands
Pink	3	1
Blue	2	1
Brimstone	1	2

DESCRIPTION

A unit of Horrors of Tzeentch has any number of models, each armed with Magical Flames and Taloned Hands.

PINK HORRORS: Any number of models in this unit can be Pink Horrors.

BLUE HORRORS: Any number of models in this unit can be Blue Horrors.

BRIMSTONE HORRORS: Any number of models in this unit can be Brimstone Horrors.

IRIDESCENT HORROR: 1 Pink Horror model in this unit can be an Iridescent Horror. Add 1 to the Attacks characteristic of that model's melee weapon.

ICON BEARER: 1 in every 10 Pink Horror models in this unit can be a Pink Horror Icon Bearer. If the unmodified roll for a battleshock test for this unit while it includes any Pink Horror Icon Bearers is 1, you can return D6 slain **HORRORS OF TZEENTCH** models to this unit, and no models from this unit will flee in that battleshock phase. Set up the **HORRORS OF TZEENTCH** models one at a time within 1" of a model from this unit that has not been returned in that phase. The models can only be set up within 3" of an enemy unit if this unit was within 3" of that enemy unit before any models were returned.

HORNBLOWER: 1 in every 10 Pink Horror models in this unit can be a Pink Horror Hornblower. If the unmodified roll for a battleshock test for an enemy unit that is within 6" of this unit while this unit includes any Pink Horror Hornblowers is 1, that battleshock test must be re-rolled.

ABILITIES

Ectoplasmic Elasticity: *The physicality of a Pink Horror can withstand enemy attacks, allowing it to reform its shape instantly.*

Roll a dice each time you allocate a wound or mortal wound to a Pink Horror from this unit. On a 6, that wound or mortal wound is negated.

Flickering Flames: *Combining their magical might, Horrors consume their enemies in maelstroms of arcane fire.*

Add 1 to hit rolls for attacks made with this unit's Magical Flames while this unit has 20 or more models.

Split and Split Again: *Should a Horror meet its end at the hands of the enemy, it is capable of splitting itself into lesser daemons and renewing its assault twice over.*

When you allocate wounds or mortal wounds to this unit, you must allocate them to a Pink Horror model if it is possible to do so.

Each time an Iridescent Horror or Pink Horror model from a friendly unit with this ability is slain, you can add 2 Blue Horror models to that unit after removing the slain model. Each time a Blue Horror model from a friendly unit with this ability is slain, you can add 1 Brimstone Horrors model to that unit after removing the slain model.

Set up the additional models one at a time within 1" of the position that the slain model had occupied. The additional models can only be set up within 3" of an enemy unit if the position that the slain model had occupied or any other models from the slain model's unit are within 3" of that enemy unit. If you cannot set up the additional models in this way, they are removed from play (they do not count as being slain).

Locus of Conjuration: *Tzeentch bolsters his Horrors by channelling eldritch energies through nearby champions.*

Add 1 to casting rolls for this unit while it is wholly within 12" of any friendly **TZEENTCH DAEMON HEROES**.

Petty Vengeance: *Some Horrors take petty vengeance on those who harm them by exploding in a blast of flame.*

If a Pink Horror model from this unit is slain and you do not use its Split and Split Again ability to add any models to this unit, you can pick 1 enemy unit within 1" of this unit and roll a dice. On a 5+, that enemy unit suffers 1 mortal wound.

MAGIC

This unit is a **WIZARD** while it has 9 or more Pink Horrors. It can attempt to cast 1 spell in your hero phase and attempt to unbind 1 spell in the enemy hero phase. It knows the Channelled Pink Fire spell. It cannot attempt to cast any spells other than Channelled Pink Fire, but any number of **HORRORS OF TZEENTCH** units that have 9 or more Pink Horrors can attempt to cast Channelled Pink Fire in the same hero phase.

Channelled Pink Fire: *As the Horrors chant verses in the Dark Tongue in unison, their pink forms illuminate, charging their magical essence.*

Channelled Pink Fire has a casting value of 6. If successfully cast, pick 1 friendly **HORRORS OF TZEENTCH** unit wholly within 6" of the caster and visible to them. Add 1 to hit rolls for attacks made by that unit until the start of your next hero phase. A unit cannot benefit from this spell more than once per phase.

KEYWORDS	CHAOS, DAEMON, HORROR, TZEENTCH, HORRORS OF TZEENTCH

108

MOVE	16"
WOUNDS	6
SAVE	5+
BRAVERY	7

MAGISTER
ON DISC OF TZEENTCH

Magisters are powerful sorcerers in service to Tzeentch. Filled with eldritch energies as they ride their Disc of Tzeentch, they can wield fantastical fires to scorch the foe or transform an enemy into the squelching, misshapen form of a Chaos Spawn.

MISSILE WEAPONS	Range	Attacks	To Hit	To Wound	Rend	Damage
Tzeentchian Runestaff	18"	1	3+	4+	-	D3
MELEE WEAPONS	Range	Attacks	To Hit	To Wound	Rend	Damage
Warpsteel Sword	1"	1	4+	4+	-	1
Teeth and Horns	1"	D3	4+	3+	-1	D3

DESCRIPTION
A Magister on Disc of Tzeentch is a single model armed with a Tzeentchian Runestaff and Warpsteel Sword.

MOUNT: This model's Disc of Tzeentch attacks with its Teeth and Horns.

FLY: This model can fly.

ABILITIES
Magic-touched: *Magisters are attuned to magical energy and can harness the raw essence of Chaos. There are those, however, that delve too deep into this source of power.*

If the casting roll for this model is a double and the casting attempt is successful and not unbound, this model can attempt to cast 1 extra spell this turn. If it does so and the extra casting roll is a double, the spell automatically fails and this model is slain.

If a friendly **MAGISTER** is slain by this effect, roll a dice before removing the model. On a 2+, 1 **TZEENTCH CHAOS SPAWN** is added to your army. Set up the **TZEENTCH CHAOS SPAWN** anywhere on the battlefield within 1" of the slain **MAGISTER** and more than 3" from any enemy units.

MAGIC
This model is a **WIZARD**. It can attempt to cast 1 spell in your hero phase and attempt to unbind 1 spell in the enemy hero phase. It knows the Arcane Bolt, Mystic Shield and Bolt of Change spells.

Bolt of Change: *The Magister hurls a coruscating bolt of energy at the foe, causing their flesh to run like wax and remould into a form more pleasing to Tzeentch.*

Bolt of Change has a casting value of 7. If successfully cast, pick 1 enemy unit within 18" of the caster and visible to them. That unit suffers D3 mortal wounds. If any models were slain by this spell, before removing the first slain model, you can add 1 **TZEENTCH CHAOS SPAWN** to your army and set it up within 3" of the slain model's unit.

| KEYWORDS | CHAOS, MORTAL, TZEENTCH, ARCANITE, HERO, WIZARD, MAGISTER |

MAGISTER

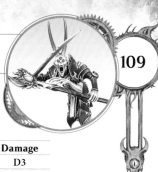

MOVE 6"
WOUNDS 5
SAVE 5+
BRAVERY 7

As a central figure of the cabal that leads an Arcanite Cult, a Magister will use all their fell powers to inflict change and ruin upon the Mortal Realms in the name of the Great Conspirator. At their hands are the enemies of Tzeentch transformed.

MISSILE WEAPONS	Range	Attacks	To Hit	To Wound	Rend	Damage
Tzeentchian Runestaff	18"	1	3+	4+	-	D3
MELEE WEAPONS	**Range**	**Attacks**	**To Hit**	**To Wound**	**Rend**	**Damage**
Warpsteel Sword	1"	1	4+	4+	-	1

DESCRIPTION

A Magister is a single model armed with a Tzeentchian Runestaff and Warpsteel Sword.

ABILITIES

Magic-touched: *Magisters are attuned to magical energy. There are those, however, that delve too deep into this source of power.*

If the casting roll for this model is a double and the casting attempt is successful and not unbound, this model can attempt to cast 1 extra spell this turn. If it does so and the extra casting roll is a double, the spell automatically fails and this model is slain. If a friendly **MAGISTER** is slain by this effect, roll a dice before removing the model. On a 2+, 1 **TZEENTCH CHAOS SPAWN** is added to your army. Set up the **TZEENTCH CHAOS SPAWN** anywhere on the battlefield within 1" of the slain **MAGISTER** and more than 3" from any enemy units.

MAGIC

This model is a **WIZARD**. It can attempt to cast 1 spell in your hero phase and attempt to unbind 1 spell in the enemy hero phase. It knows the Arcane Bolt, Mystic Shield and Bolt of Change spells.

Bolt of Change: *The Magister hurls a coruscating bolt of energy at the foe.*

Bolt of Change has a casting value of 7. If successfully cast, pick 1 enemy unit within 18" of the caster and visible to them. That unit suffers D3 mortal wounds. If any models were slain by this spell, before removing the first slain model, you can add 1 **TZEENTCH CHAOS SPAWN** to your army and set it up within 3" of the slain model's unit.

KEYWORDS	CHAOS, MORTAL, TZEENTCH, ARCANITE, HERO, WIZARD, MAGISTER

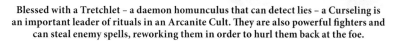

CURSELING
EYE OF TZEENTCH

MOVE 5"
WOUNDS 5
SAVE 4+
BRAVERY 7

Blessed with a Tretchlet – a daemon homunculus that can detect lies – a Curseling is an important leader of rituals in an Arcanite Cult. They are also powerful fighters and can steal enemy spells, reworking them in order to hurl them back at the foe.

MELEE WEAPONS	Range	Attacks	To Hit	To Wound	Rend	Damage
Blazing Sword	1"	3	3+	4+	-1	1
Threshing Flail	1"	3	4+	3+	-	1
Staff of Tzeentch	2"	1	5+	4+	-	D3

DESCRIPTION

A Curseling, Eye of Tzeentch, is a single model armed with a Blazing Sword, Threshing Flail and Staff of Tzeentch.

ABILITIES

Disrupter of the Arcane: *A Curseling can reach into a spell and undo the magical forces that keep it whole.*

You can re-roll unbinding and dispelling rolls for this model.

Vessel of Chaos: *The flow of eldritch energy is visible to the Curseling, who can pluck magic from the aether and hurl it back at its caster.*

If this model successfully unbinds a spell that is possible for it to cast, it can immediately attempt to cast that spell even though it is the enemy hero phase. If that spell is successfully cast, it cannot be unbound.

MAGIC

This model is a **WIZARD**. It can attempt to cast 2 spells in your hero phase and attempt to unbind 2 spells in the enemy hero phase. It knows the Arcane Bolt, Mystic Shield and Glean Magic spells.

Glean Magic: *In a magical duel, the Curseling reaches into his adversary's mind and steals arcane knowledge to use for his own ends.*

Glean Magic has a casting value of 3. If successfully cast, pick 1 enemy **WIZARD** within 24" of the caster and visible to them. Pick 1 spell from that **WIZARD**'s warscroll that is possible for this model to cast and roll a dice. On a 3+, the caster knows that spell for the rest of the battle.

KEYWORDS	CHAOS, MORTAL, TZEENTCH, ARCANITE, HERO, WIZARD, CURSELING

110

MOVE **6"**
WOUNDS **1**
SAVE **6+**
BRAVERY **6**

THE EYES OF THE NINE

Agents of the Gaunt Summoners, the Eyes of the Nine seek out artefacts redolent with realm magics that they can corrupt with Tzeentchian energy. With these ensorcelled lodestones, they intend to tether the Silver Towers to reality.

MISSILE WEAPONS	Range	Attacks	To Hit	To Wound	Rend	Damage
Magical Flames	12"	2	5+	4+	-	1
Sorcerous Bolt	12"	1	5+	4+	-	1
MELEE WEAPONS	Range	Attacks	To Hit	To Wound	Rend	Damage
Savage Greatblade	1"	1	4+	4+	-1	2
Cursed Blade	1"	1	4+	4+	-	1
Vicious Beak	1"	1	4+	5+	-	1
Taloned Hands	1"	1	5+	4+	-	1

DESCRIPTION

The Eyes of the Nine is a unit that has 4 models. Narvia and Turosh are each armed with a Cursed Blade, Sorcerous Bolt and Arcanite Shield; K'charik is armed with a Savage Greatblade and Vicious Beak; and the Blue Horror is armed with Magical Flames and Taloned Hands.

K'CHARIK: Add 1 to K'charik's Wounds characteristic.

ABILITIES

Arcanite Shield: *This shield can protect against both physical and magical attacks.*

Roll a dice each time you allocate a wound or mortal wound to a unit that has any models armed with Arcanite Shields. On a 6, that wound or mortal wound is negated.

Split: *If the Blue Horror is slain, it transforms into a pair of Brimstone Horrors.*

If the Blue Horror model from a friendly unit with this ability is slain, you can add 1 Brimstone Horrors model to that unit after removing the slain model. The Brimstone Horrors' Magical Flames have an Attacks characteristic of 1 instead of 2, and their Taloned Hands have an Attacks characteristic of 2 instead of 1.

KEYWORDS	CHAOS, TZEENTCH, CULT OF THE TRANSIENT FORM, EYES OF THE NINE

MOVE **6"**
WOUNDS **5**
SAVE **5+**
BRAVERY **7**

VORTEMIS THE ALL-SEEING

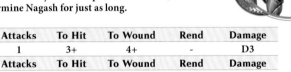

Vortemis has been instrumental in twisting the strands of fate to serve the will of Tzeentch. His Arcanite Cult had spies in the city of Shadespire for centuries, and he has plotted to undermine Nagash for just as long.

MISSILE WEAPONS	Range	Attacks	To Hit	To Wound	Rend	Damage
Tzeentchian Runestaff	18"	1	3+	4+	-	D3
MELEE WEAPONS	Range	Attacks	To Hit	To Wound	Rend	Damage
Tzeentchian Runestaff	1"	1	4+	4+	-	1

DESCRIPTION

Vortemis the All-seeing is a named character that is a single model. He is armed with a Tzeentchian Runestaff.

ABILITIES

Magic-touched: *Magisters are attuned to magical energy like no other, but there are those that delve too deep into this source of power.*

If the casting roll for this model is a double and the casting attempt is successful and not unbound, this model can attempt to cast 1 extra spell this turn. If it does so and the extra casting roll is a double, the spell automatically fails and this model is slain. If a friendly **MAGISTER** is slain by this effect, roll a dice before removing the model. On a 2+, 1 **TZEENTCH CHAOS SPAWN** is added to your army. Set up the **TZEENTCH CHAOS SPAWN** anywhere on the battlefield within 1" of the slain **MAGISTER** and more than 3" from any enemy units.

MAGIC

Vortemis the All-seeing is a **WIZARD**. He can attempt to cast 1 spell in your hero phase and attempt to unbind 1 spell in the enemy hero phase. He knows the Arcane Bolt, Mystic Shield and Sorcerous Insight spells.

Sorcerous Insight: *Memory becomes echo, echo becomes resonance, resonance becomes reality wrought anew.*

Sorcerous Insight has a casting value of 5. If successfully cast, you receive 1 extra command point. This extra command point can only be spent by picking this model to use the At the Double, Forward to Victory or Inspiring Presence command ability.

KEYWORDS	CHAOS, MORTAL, TZEENTCH, ARCANITE, CULT OF THE TRANSIENT FORM, HERO, WIZARD, MAGISTER, VORTEMIS THE ALL-SEEING

MOVE	16"
WOUNDS	6
SAVE	4+
BRAVERY	8

FATEMASTER

More than just a powerful warrior, a Fatemaster is surrounded by an aura of change. Mounted atop Discs of Tzeentch, Fatemasters streak into combat, slicing foes with their fireglaives while manipulating fortune for the benefit of their Arcanite Cult.

MELEE WEAPONS	Range	Attacks	To Hit	To Wound	Rend	Damage
Fireglaive of Tzeentch	2"	3	3+	4+	-	D3
Teeth and Horns	1"	D3	4+	3+	-1	D3

DESCRIPTION

A Fatemaster is a single model armed with a Fireglaive of Tzeentch.

MOUNT: This model's Disc of Tzeentch attacks with its Teeth and Horns.

FLY: This model can fly.

ABILITIES

Hovering Disc of Tzeentch: *A Fatemaster mounted on a Disc of Tzeentch is capable of truly breathtaking feats of agility and evasion.*

Add 2 to save rolls for attacks made with melee weapons that target this model unless the attacking unit is a **Monster** or can fly.

Soulbound Shield: *This shield can shelter the wielder against even the most potent magical attacks.*

Each time this model is affected by a spell or endless spell, you can roll a dice. If you do so, on a 4+, ignore the effects of that spell or endless spell on this model.

COMMAND ABILITY

Lord of Fate: *Tzeentch's chosen disciples can affect the destiny of those around them.*

You can use this command ability at the start of your hero phase. If you do so, pick a friendly model with this command ability. Until your next hero phase, you can re-roll hit rolls for attacks made by friendly **Tzeentch** units wholly within 9" of this model.

KEYWORDS	CHAOS, MORTAL, TZEENTCH, ARCANITE, HERO, FATEMASTER

MOVE	6"
WOUNDS	8
SAVE	5+
BRAVERY	8

OGROID THAUMATURGE

Combining bestial strength with dark occult powers, the Ogroid Thaumaturge is a deadly foe. With snarled invocations, it hurls blasts of fiery energy into the enemy ranks, before stampeding into their midst to pummel the survivors to bloody ruin.

MELEE WEAPONS	Range	Attacks	To Hit	To Wound	Rend	Damage
Great Horns	1"	2	3+	3+	-2	3
Thaumaturge Staff	2"	3	3+	3+	-1	D3
Cloven Hooves	1"	4	4+	3+	-	1

DESCRIPTION

An Ogroid Thaumaturge is a single model armed with Great Horns, Thaumaturge Staff and Cloven Hooves.

ABILITIES

Brutal Rage: *When wounded, the Ogroid finds bursts of renewed energy from its rage.*

You can re-roll hit and wound rolls for attacks made with melee weapons by this model if any wounds or mortal wounds were allocated to this model earlier in the same phase.

Mighty Rampage: *There are few things as deadly as the momentum of an Ogroid Thaumaturge on the charge.*

After this model makes a charge move, you can pick 1 enemy unit within 1" of this model and roll a dice. On a 2+, that unit suffers D3 mortal wounds.

MAGIC

This model is a **Wizard**. It can attempt to cast 1 spell in your hero phase and attempt to unbind 1 spell in the enemy hero phase. It knows the Arcane Bolt, Mystic Shield and Choking Tendrils spells.

Choking Tendrils: *The caster unleashes lashes of arcane energy that strangle the life from their victims.*

Choking Tendrils has a casting value of 7. If successfully cast, pick 1 enemy unit within 18" of the caster and visible to them. That unit suffers D6 mortal wounds. For each model that is slain by mortal wounds inflicted by this spell, you can heal 1 wound allocated to this model.

KEYWORDS	CHAOS, MORTAL, TZEENTCH, ARCANITE, HERO, WIZARD, OGROID THAUMATURGE

KAIRIC ACOLYTES

Kairic Acolytes are the chosen human cultists of Tzeentch. Harnessing their collective
magical might, the Chanters of Change unleash it in the form of searing bolts.
Enemies that do not fall before this arcane fusillade must face their curved blades.

MISSILE WEAPONS	Range	Attacks	To Hit	To Wound	Rend	Damage
Sorcerous Bolt	18"	1	4+	3+	-	1
MELEE WEAPONS	**Range**	**Attacks**	**To Hit**	**To Wound**	**Rend**	**Damage**
Cursed Glaive	1"	1	4+	3+	-1	2
Cursed Blade(s)	1"	1	4+	3+	-	1

DESCRIPTION

A unit of Kairic Acolytes has any number of
models. The unit is armed with Sorcerous
Bolts and one of the following weapon options:
Cursed Blade and Arcanite Shield; or a pair of
Cursed Blades.

3 in every 10 models in this unit can replace their
weapon option with a Cursed Glaive.

KAIRIC ADEPT: 1 model in this unit can be a
Kairic Adept. Add 1 to the Attacks characteristic
of that model's melee weapons.

SCROLL OF DARK ARTS: 1 in every 10
models in this unit can carry a Scroll of Dark
Arts. A unit that includes any Scrolls of Dark
Arts can add 1 to casting and unbinding rolls.

VULCHARC: 1 in every 10 models in this unit
can be accompanied by a Vulcharc. If an enemy
WIZARD successfully casts a spell within 18"
of a friendly unit that includes any Vulcharcs,
roll a dice. On a 4+, that **WIZARD** suffers 1
mortal wound after the effects of that spell have
been resolved.

ABILITIES

Arcanite Shields: *This lavishly wrought
shield can protect against both physical and
magical attacks.*

Roll a dice each time you allocate a wound or
mortal wound to a unit that has any models
armed with Arcanite Shields. On a 6, that wound
or mortal wound is negated. When you allocate
wounds or mortal wounds to this unit, you must
allocate them to a model armed with an Arcanite
Shield if it is possible to do so.

Paired Cursed Blades: *Those who wield twin
cursed blades can strong-arm enemy weapons
aside for a cleaner strike.*

You can re-roll hit rolls for attacks made with a
pair of Cursed Blades.

MAGIC

This unit is a **WIZARD** while it has 9 or more
models. It can attempt to cast 1 spell in your
hero phase and attempt to unbind 1 spell in the
enemy hero phase. It knows the Gestalt Sorcery
spell. It cannot attempt to cast any spells other
than Gestalt Sorcery, but any number of **KAIRIC
ACOLYTES** units can attempt to cast Gestalt
Sorcery in the same hero phase.

Gestalt Sorcery: *Through combined worship, a
cult of Acolytes can swell their arcane power to
new levels of ferocity.*

Gestalt Sorcery has a casting value of 6. If
successfully cast, pick 1 friendly **KAIRIC
ACOLYTES** unit wholly within 9" of the caster.
Until your next hero phase, improve the Rend
characteristic of that unit's Sorcerous Bolt attack
by 1. A unit cannot benefit from this spell more
than once per turn.

KEYWORDS	CHAOS, MORTAL, TZEENTCH, ARCANITE, KAIRIC ACOLYTES

TZAANGOR SKYFIRES

113

Tzaangor Skyfires soar across the battlefield, raining death upon the foe. Able to catch glimpses of the future, the Skyfires send their Arrows of Fate on baffling trajectories, striking their targets' most vulnerable weak spots with confounding accuracy.

MOVE **16"**
WOUNDS **4**
SAVE **5+**
BRAVERY **6**

MISSILE WEAPONS	Range	Attacks	To Hit	To Wound	Rend	Damage
Arrow of Fate	24"	1	4+	3+	-1	D3
MELEE WEAPONS	Range	Attacks	To Hit	To Wound	Rend	Damage
Bow Stave	1"	2	5+	5+	-	1
Vicious Beak	1"	1	4+	5+	-	1
Teeth and Horns	1"	D3	4+	3+	-1	D3

DESCRIPTION

A unit of Tzaangor Skyfires has any number of models, each armed with an Arrow of Fate, Bow Stave and Vicious Beak.

MOUNT: This unit's Discs of Tzeentch attack with their Teeth and Horns.

AVIARCH: The leader of this unit is an Aviarch. Add 1 to hit rolls for attacks made with an Aviarch's Arrow of Fate.

FLY: This unit can fly.

ABILITIES

Guided by the Future: *These warriors' attacks are directed by glimpses of the future.*

In the combat phase, you can re-roll hit and wound rolls for attacks made by this unit if no enemy units within 3" of this unit have already fought in that phase.

Judgement from Afar: *To be struck by an Arrow of Fate is to be judged by destiny itself.*

If the unmodified hit roll for an attack made with an Arrow of Fate is 6, that attack inflicts D3 mortal wounds on the target and the attack sequence ends (do not make a wound or save roll).

KEYWORDS	CHAOS, GOR, BEASTS OF CHAOS, BRAYHERD, TZEENTCH, ARCANITE, TZAANGOR SKYFIRES

TZEENTCH CHAOS SPAWN

Tzeentch Chaos Spawn are, if anything, even more horrifically mutated than others of their kind. Altered at the whim of the Great Mutator, they tear their prey limb from limb with their freakish array of claws, tentacles and hooked appendages.

MOVE **2D6"**
WOUNDS **5**
SAVE **5+**
BRAVERY **10**

MELEE WEAPONS	Range	Attacks	To Hit	To Wound	Rend	Damage
Freakish Mutations	1"	2D6	4+	4+	-	1

DESCRIPTION

A unit of Tzeentch Chaos Spawn has any number of models, each armed with Freakish Mutations.

ABILITIES

Writhing Tentacles: *The body of a Chaos Spawn is ever in flux, making them wildly unpredictable adversaries.*

If you roll a double when determining the number of attacks made by Freakish Mutations, add 1 to hit and wound rolls for attacks made by the attacking model until the end of the phase.

KEYWORDS	CHAOS, MORTAL, TZEENTCH, SLAVES TO DARKNESS, CHAOS SPAWN

114

MOVE **16"**

WOUNDS **6**

SAVE **5+**

6

BRAVERY

TZAANGOR SHAMAN

Mounted atop a Disc of Tzeentch, a Tzaangor Shaman is a potent agent of change. With dark magics, the Shaman will grant a boon of mutation to his foes, transforming them as they writhe and scream into a more pleasing form – that of a Tzaangor.

MELEE WEAPONS	Range	Attacks	To Hit	To Wound	Rend	Damage
Staff of Change	2"	1	4+	3+	-1	D3
Ritual Dagger	1"	2	4+	4+	-	1
Teeth and Horns	1"	D3	4+	3+	-1	D3

DESCRIPTION

A Tzaangor Shaman is a single model armed with a Staff of Change and Ritual Dagger.

MOUNT: This model's Disc of Tzeentch attacks with its Teeth and Horns.

FLY: This model can fly.

ABILITIES

Sorcerous Elixir: *Tzaangor Shamans drink strange concoctions in battle to augment their sorcerous might.*

Once per battle, in your hero phase, this model can attempt to cast 1 extra spell. If it does so, you can re-roll the casting roll for that spell.

Visions of the Future: *Seeing the battle unfold before them through prophetic visions, the Shaman guides the aim of nearby Tzaangor Skyfires.*

Add 1 to hit rolls for attacks made with Arrows of Fate by friendly **TZAANGOR SKYFIRE** units wholly within 12" of any friendly **TZAANGOR SHAMANS**.

Visions of the Past: *By listing the weaknesses of the foe discovered in ages past, Tzaangor Shamans enhance the deadliness of their Enlightened kin.*

Add 1 to hit rolls for attacks made with Tzeentchian Spears and Vicious Beaks by friendly **TZAANGOR ENLIGHTENED** units wholly within 12" of any friendly **TZAANGOR SHAMANS**.

MAGIC

This model is a **WIZARD**. It can attempt to cast 1 spell in your hero phase and attempt to unbind 1 spell in the enemy hero phase. It knows the Arcane Bolt, Mystic Shield and Boon of Mutation spells.

Boon of Mutation: *The Shaman curses its foes with the dubious gift of Tzeentch's mutagenic power, transforming its victims into a form more pleasing to the Changer of the Ways.*

Boon of Mutation has a casting value of 7. If successfully cast, pick an enemy unit within 18" of the caster and visible to them. That unit suffers D3 mortal wounds. For each model that is slain by mortal wounds inflicted by this spell, you can add 1 **TZAANGOR** model to an existing **TZAANGOR** unit in your army. If you do so, set up that **TZAANGOR** model within 1" of a friendly **TZAANGOR** unit that is within 12" of the caster. The model can only be set up within 3" of an enemy unit if the friendly unit was within 3" of that enemy unit before any models were added.

KEYWORDS	CHAOS, GOR, BEASTS OF CHAOS, BRAYHERD, TZEENTCH, ARCANITE, HERO, WIZARD, TZAANGOR SHAMAN

TZAANGOR ENLIGHTENED

MOVE 6"
WOUNDS 3
SAVE 5+
BRAVERY 6

Tzaangor Enlightened are arrogant creatures, for they can see the lessons of the past as easily as mortals see daylight. They gleefully caw out the past mistakes of their enemies, unnerving them before moving in to capitalise with each blow.

MELEE WEAPONS	Range	Attacks	To Hit	To Wound	Rend	Damage
Tzeentchian Spear	2"	3	4+	3+	-1	2
Vicious Beak	1"	1	4+	5+	-	1

DESCRIPTION

A unit of Tzaangor Enlightened has any number of models, each armed with a Tzeentchian Spear and Vicious Beak.

AVIARCH: The leader of this unit is an Aviarch. Add 1 to the Attacks characteristic of an Aviarch's Tzeentchian Spear.

ABILITIES

Babbling Stream of Secrets: *The dark truths revealed by the Tzaangor Enlightened utterly unnerve the foe.*

If an enemy unit fails a battleshock test within 9" of any friendly **Tzaangor Enlightened** units, add 1 to the number of models that flee.

Guided by the Past: *These warriors see at once every moment that led to the present and use this knowledge to deadly effect.*

In the combat phase, you can re-roll hit and wound rolls for attacks made by this unit if any enemy units within 3" of this unit have already fought in that phase.

KEYWORDS	CHAOS, GOR, BEASTS OF CHAOS, BRAYHERD, TZEENTCH, ARCANITE, TZAANGOR ENLIGHTENED

TZAANGOR ENLIGHTENED
ON DISCS OF TZEENTCH

MOVE 16"
WOUNDS 4
SAVE 5+
BRAVERY 6

Tzaangor Enlightened wield ornate spears of a quality beyond the weaponry of their lesser kin. Able to perceive the strands of the past, the Enlightened reveal the hidden secrets of their foes, discovering their weaknesses before moving in to strike.

MELEE WEAPONS	Range	Attacks	To Hit	To Wound	Rend	Damage
Tzeentchian Spear	2"	3	4+	3+	-1	2
Vicious Beak	1"	1	4+	5+	-	1
Teeth and Horns	1"	D3	4+	3+	-1	D3

DESCRIPTION

A unit of Tzaangor Enlightened has any number of models, each armed with a Tzeentchian Spear and Vicious Beak.

MOUNT: This unit's Discs of Tzeentch attack with their Teeth and Horns.

AVIARCH: The leader of this unit is an Aviarch. Add 1 to the Attacks characteristic of an Aviarch's Tzeentchian Spear.

FLY: This unit can fly.

ABILITIES

Babbling Stream of Secrets: *The dark truths revealed by the Tzaangor Enlightened utterly unnerve the foe.*

If an enemy unit fails a battleshock test within 9" of any friendly **Tzaangor Enlightened** units, add 1 to the number of models that flee.

Guided by the Past: *These warriors see at once every moment that led to the present and use this knowledge to deadly effect.*

In the combat phase, you can re-roll hit and wound rolls for attacks made by this unit if any enemy units within 3" of this unit have already fought in that phase.

KEYWORDS	CHAOS, GOR, BEASTS OF CHAOS, BRAYHERD, TZEENTCH, ARCANITE, TZAANGOR ENLIGHTENED

TZAANGORS

MOVE 6"
WOUNDS 2
SAVE 5+
BRAVERY 5

116

Tzaangors are savage, avian beastmen dedicated to Tzeentch and gifted with his dark blessings. Eager to impress their duplicitous god, the Tzaangors fight with lunatic energies, hoping to earn further gifts of change.

MELEE WEAPONS	Range	Attacks	To Hit	To Wound	Rend	Damage
Savage Greatblade	1"	1	4+	4+	-1	2
Savage Blade(s)	1"	2	4+	4+	-	1
Vicious Beak	1"	1	4+	5+	-	1

DESCRIPTION

A unit of Tzaangors has any number of models. The unit is armed with a Vicious Beak and one of the following weapon options: Savage Blade and Arcanite Shield; or a pair of Savage Blades. 2 in every 5 models can replace their weapon option with a Savage Greatblade.

TWISTBRAY: 1 model in this unit can be a Twistbray. Add 1 to hit rolls for attacks made with that model's melee weapons.

TZAANGOR MUTANT: 1 in every 5 models in this unit can be a Tzaangor Mutant armed with a pair of Savage Blades and a Vicious Beak. Add 1 to the Attacks characteristic of that model's pair of Savage Blades.

ICON BEARER: 1 in every 10 models in this unit can be an Icon Bearer. A unit that includes any Icon Bearers can use the Ornate Totems ability.

BRAYHORN: 1 in every 10 models in this unit can have a Brayhorn. A unit that includes any Brayhorns can run and still charge later in the same turn.

ABILITIES

Destined Mayhem: *Nearby leaders and champions of the Arcanites inspire Tzaangors to deliver killing blows to the enemy.*

Add 1 to wound rolls for attacks made with melee weapons by this unit while this unit is wholly within 12" of any friendly **ARCANITE HEROES**.

Arcanite Shield: *This lavishly wrought shield can protect against both physical and magical attacks.*

Roll a dice each time you allocate a wound or mortal wound to a unit that has any models armed with Arcanite Shields. On a 6, that wound or mortal wound is negated. When you allocate wounds or mortal wounds to this unit, you must allocate them to a model armed with an Arcanite Shield if it is possible to do so.

Paired Savage Blades: *Tzaangors armed with two savage blades have a better chance of landing a blow on the enemy.*

Add 1 to hit rolls for attacks made with a pair of Savage Blades.

Savagery Unleashed: *Favoured by their god, these warriors unleash a flurry of attacks upon their foes.*

Add 1 to the Attacks characteristic of this unit's melee weapons while it has 9 or more models.

Ornate Totems: *The icons carried by the Tzaangors can steal magical power from nearby wizards and use it to blast the enemy.*

While this unit has 1 or more Icon Bearers, at the start of your hero phase, you can pick 1 enemy unit within 18" of this unit that is visible to it. Roll 1 dice for each **WIZARD** that is within 9" of this unit. For each 4+, that unit suffers 1 mortal wound.

KEYWORDS | CHAOS, GOR, BEASTS OF CHAOS, BRAYHERD, TZEENTCH, ARCANITE, TZAANGORS

BURNING SIGIL OF TZEENTCH

Drizzling ectoplasm and daemonic fire, the conjured sigil of Tzeentch is so redolent with mutative energies that it can transform those around it into a thousand fleshy forms. To stand close by is to risk horrific transmogrification – though in the final reckoning of battle, some of these mutations are as much a blessing as they are a curse.

DESCRIPTION

A Burning Sigil of Tzeentch is a single model.

MAGIC

Summon Burning Sigil of Tzeentch: *Brief incantations in the Dark Tongue see these burning symbols of worship spark into reality.*

Summon Burning Sigil of Tzeentch has a casting value of 5. Only **Tzeentch Wizards** can attempt to cast this spell. If successfully cast, set up 1 Burning Sigil of Tzeentch model wholly within 18" of the caster.

ABILITIES

Radiant Transmogrification: *The sigil channels the energies of the Impossible Fortress; with each pulse comes a handful of blessings and curses as fickle as the bastion's master.*

At the end of your movement phase, if the Burning Sigil of Tzeentch is on the battlefield, you must roll a dice on the following table:

D6	Effect
1	**Dismembered by Change:** Pick 1 unit within 12" of this model and visible to it. That unit suffers D3 mortal wounds. If any models were slain by this spell, before removing the first slain model, you can add 1 **Tzeentch Chaos Spawn** to your army and set it up within 3" of the slain model's unit.
2	**Crippling Appendages:** Pick 1 unit within 12" of this model and visible to it. Halve the Move characteristic of that unit until the start of your next hero phase.
3-4	**Mutative Flux:** Pick 1 unit within 12" of this model and visible to it. That unit can move D6" even if it ran in the same turn.
5	**Spawning Limbs:** Pick 1 unit within 12" of this model and visible to it. Add 1 to the Attacks characteristic of that unit's melee weapons until the start of your next hero phase.
6	**Shifting Aura:** Pick 1 unit within 12" of this model and visible to it. Subtract 1 from hit rolls for attacks that target that unit until the start of your next hero phase.

KEYWORDS	ENDLESS SPELL, BURNING SIGIL OF TZEENTCH

TOME OF EYES

By conjuring a Tome of Eyes, a spellcaster can read knowledge inscribed by daemonic forces as the tome reads them in turn; in doing so, they gain access to the fabled Parchment Curse. A particularly disturbing spell, this turns the enemies of the caster into scattering sheafs of paper, each detailing a dark and twisted version of the victim's life story.

DESCRIPTION

A Tome of Eyes is a single model.

MAGIC

Summon Tome of Eyes: *With a snap of the conjurer's fingers, the Tome appears at their side from a spark of blue wyrdflame.*

Summon Tome of Eyes has a casting value of 5. Only **Tzeentch Wizards** can attempt to cast this spell. If successfully cast, set up 1 Tome of Eyes model within 1" of the caster.

As long as the Tome of Eyes is on the battlefield, the caster and the Tome of Eyes are treated as being a single model from the caster's army that uses the caster's warscroll as well as the Endless Spells rules. The Tome of Eyes must remain within 1" of the caster. If the caster is slain, then the Tome of Eyes is immediately dispelled and removed from play along with the caster.

The Parchment Curse: *The Tome's flames intensify, its eyes twitching frantically as it seeks new prey for the curses on its parchment leaves.*

The Parchment Curse has a casting value of 8. Only the caster of the Tome of Eyes can attempt to cast this spell. If successfully cast, pick 1 enemy unit within 18" of the caster that is visible to them and roll a dice. On a 3+, that unit suffers D3 mortal wounds. In addition, for each model that is slain by mortal wounds inflicted by this spell, subtract 1 from the Bravery characteristic of that unit for the rest of the battle.

ABILITIES

Transfixed by Countless Eyes: *As the Tome flicks through its endless pages, it peers into the mind of its summoner, giving knowledge to the loyal and punishing the insatiable as it sees fit.*

If the Tome of Eyes is on the battlefield, you can re-roll casting rolls for the caster.

In addition, if the unmodified casting roll for a spell attempted by the caster is a 2 or a 12, the spell is automatically cast (regardless of the result) and cannot be unbound. However, the caster suffers D3 mortal wounds after the effects of that spell have been resolved.

KEYWORDS	ENDLESS SPELL, TOME OF EYES

DAEMONIC SIMULACRUM

The twin-headed monstrosity known as the Daemonic Simulacrum is not a true daemon but a living mirage, a manifestation of the duplicity and cunning of the Lords of Change that guide their Arcanite puppets to war. Though ephemeral, when these illusory creatures bite, they can tear away the minds of the foe to leave them drooling imbeciles.

DESCRIPTION

A Daemonic Simulacrum is a single model.

PREDATORY: A Daemonic Simulacrum is a predatory endless spell. It can move up to 9" and can fly.

MAGIC

Summon Daemonic Simulacrum: *The wizard draws upon its understanding of Changelore to create a temporary portal for this mirage to enter the fray.*

Summon Daemonic Simulacrum has a casting value of 7. Only **Tzeentch Wizards** can attempt to cast this spell. If successfully cast, set up 1 Daemonic Simulacrum model wholly within 12" of the caster.

ABILITIES

Twisting Mirage: *This Tzeentchian manifestation writhes across the battlefield as soon as it materialises.*

When this model is set up, the player who set it up can immediately make a move with it.

Snapping Jaws: *The Simulacrum feeds upon the minds of any beings in its path and is especially drawn to sources of the arcane.*

After this model has moved, roll 9 dice for the closest other unit within 6". If more than 1 other unit is equally close, the player that moved this model can choose which unit to roll the 9 dice for. For each 5+, that unit suffers 1 mortal wound. If that unit is a **Wizard**, that unit suffers 1 mortal wound for each 4+ instead.

KEYWORDS	ENDLESS SPELL, DAEMONIC SIMULACRUM

The reality-warping spells of the Arcanum Optimar scar the air itself as the Disciples of Tzeentch summon them to the battlefield. Even to witness them is to risk one's sanity – those who become their prey are damned to an unusual and terrifying demise.

PITCHED BATTLE PROFILES

The table below provides points, minimum and maximum unit sizes and battlefield roles for the warscrolls and warscroll battalions in this book, for use in Pitched Battles. Spending the points listed in this table allows you to take a minimum-sized unit with any of its upgrades. Understrength units cost the full amount of points. Larger units are taken in multiples of their minimum unit size; multiply their cost by the same amount as you multiplied their size. If a unit has two points values separated by a slash (e.g. '60/200'), the second value is for a maximum-sized unit. Units that are listed as 'Unique' are named characters and can only be taken once in an army. A unit that has any of the keywords listed in the Allies table can be taken as an allied unit by a Tzeentch army. Updated January 2020; the profiles printed here take precedence over any profiles with an earlier publication date or no publication date.

DISCIPLES OF TZEENTCH UNIT	UNIT SIZE MIN	MAX	POINTS	BATTLEFIELD ROLE	NOTES
Horrors of Tzeentch	10	20	200	Battleline if this unit contains no Blue Horrors or Brimstone Horrors	If this unit contains no Pink Horrors, change the points cost to 100. If the unit contains no Pink Horrors and no Blue Horrors, change the points cost to 60.
Kairic Acolytes	10	30	100	Battleline	
Tzaangors	10	30	180	Battleline	
The Blue Scribes	1	1	120	Leader	Unique
Changecaster, Herald of Tzeentch	1	1	110	Leader	
The Changeling	1	1	120	Leader	Unique
Curseling, Eye of Tzeentch	1	1	160	Leader	
Fatemaster	1	1	120	Leader	
Fateskimmer, Herald of Tzeentch on Burning Chariot	1	1	140	Leader	
Fluxmaster, Herald of Tzeentch on Disc	1	1	130	Leader	
Gaunt Summoner of Tzeentch	1	1	240	Leader	
Magister	1	1	100	Leader	
Magister on Disc of Tzeentch	1	1	140	Leader	
Ogroid Thaumaturge	1	1	160	Leader	
Tzaangor Shaman	1	1	150	Leader	
Vortemis the All-seeing	1	1		Leader	Unique. These units must be taken as a set for a total of 140 points. Although taken as a set, each is a separate unit.
The Eyes of the Nine	4	4	140		
Kairos Fateweaver	1	1	400	Leader, Behemoth	Unique
Lord of Change	1	1	380	Leader, Behemoth	
Burning Chariots of Tzeentch	1	3	150		Battleline if general is a **FATESKIMMER**
Exalted Flamers of Tzeentch	1	6	100		
Flamers of Tzeentch	3	12	120		Battleline in **ETERNAL CONFLAGRATION** army
Screamers of Tzeentch	3	12	80		Battleline in **HOSTS ARCANUM** army
Tzaangor Enlightened	3	9	100		
Tzaangor Enlightened on Discs of Tzeentch	3	9	180		
Tzaangor Skyfires	3	9	200		
Tzeentch Chaos Spawn	1	6	50		

DISCIPLES OF TZEENTCH WARSCROLL	UNIT SIZE		POINTS	BATTLEFIELD ROLE	NOTES
	MIN	MAX			
Aether-eater Host	-	-	140	Warscroll Battalion	
Alter-kin Coven	-	-	140	Warscroll Battalion	
Arcanite Cabal	-	-	140	Warscroll Battalion	
Arcanite Cult	-	-	80	Warscroll Battalion	
Changehost	-	-	180	Warscroll Battalion	
Fate Legion	-	-	80	Warscroll Battalion	
Multitudinous Host	-	-	160	Warscroll Battalion	
Omniscient Oracles	-	-	160	Warscroll Battalion	
Overseer's Fate-twisters	-	-	160	Warscroll Battalion	
Skyshoal Coven	-	-	140	Warscroll Battalion	
Tzaangor Coven	-	-	180	Warscroll Battalion	
Warpflame Host	-	-	140	Warscroll Battalion	
Witchfyre Coven	-	-	160	Warscroll Battalion	
Burning Sigil of Tzeentch	1	1	40	Endless Spell	
Tome of Eyes	1	1	40	Endless Spell	
Daemonic Simulacrum	1	1	50	Endless Spell	

FACTION	ALLIES
Tzeentch	Beasts of Chaos (excluding **Nurgle** units), Monsters of Chaos, Slaanesh, Slaves to Darkness (excluding units with mark of **Nurgle**)